THE COLORS of FAITH

Our Never-Ending Spiritual Journey

W. KIRK REED

Copyright © 2021 by W. Kirk Reed

All rights reseved. No part of this publication may be reproduced, distributed, or transmitted in any form or by any means, including photocopying, recording, or other electronic or mechanical methods, without the prior written permission of the author.

ISBN:

Book cover and interior design by TeaBerryCreative.com

Contents

Chapter 1. From Black and White to Living Color · · · · · · · · · · · · · · · · 1
Chapter 2. PURPLE ·13
Chapter 3. WHITE ·35
Chapter 4. GREEN· ·59
Chapter 5. RED · 83
Chapter 6. Small, Big, and Great Questions· · · · · · · · · · · · · · · · · · · 103
Acknowledgements ·119

Chapter 1. From Black and White to Living Color

This is a book about colors. It's also about a living, vibrant faith. If you are drawn to the Christian faith, you'll experience four colors that provide for all of us a spiritual map. The colors are not the familiar primary colors—red, yellow, and blue—of everyday life. As followers of Jesus, we tell our story using the four theological colors:

1. Purple—the color of confusion and pain
2. White—the color of new beginnings and joy
3. Green—the color of growing as a follower of Jesus and changing the world
4. Red—the color of God's Holy Spirit, which makes all things possible

The four colors can help us understand the Biblical story, from Genesis to Revelation. They can also guide us in our personal journey of faith.

My hope is that this small book can help to bring our Biblical and theological heritage to life. The result can be a greater sense of serenity and well-being as we organize carpools and pay the bills and struggle with deadlines and cheer for sports teams and wonder, "What's it all about?" The colors of faith can also help us live more consciously, aware of life's Great Questions, when we are tempted to "zone out." They can stir us to be active servants of Christ in the world. They can give us clear and helpful ways to communicate, "What does it mean to be a Christian?"

The four colors of faith—purple, white, green, and red—are vivid. They are memorable. They can touch the heart as they stimulate the mind.

Is the information in this book new? Not at all. The colors of the Christian faith have been part of our heritage since the early centuries of the Common Era. But in presenting the four theological colors, I hope to offer a timely and useful outline, encouraging all of us to become more theologically literate and more Biblically grounded.[1]

---

[1] There are many variations in how liturgical colors are used. In some traditions there are days of blue or pink or black. In other traditions red is used frequently instead of sparingly. Some churches allow individual Sundays—not seasons of the Christian year—to guide the choice of colors. For many reasons I am using only four colors. First, the four-color tradition is well-established in the United Methodist Church, where my understanding of the seasons has been shaped. Second, some of the extra colors (especially blue during Advent) are derived from long-established colors. Although the new colors can be meaningful additions, they are secondary in my view. Third, the three basic colors—purple, white, and green—tell the Christian story (and our personal stories) in a way that is compelling and memorable. They also bring to life the three all-important emphases in the theology of John Wesley, as outlined by Albert C. Outler in his *Theology in the Wesleyan Spirit* (Nashville: Tidings, 1975). It's important to note that the red of Pentecost is not one of the three basic colors. It symbolizes the power of God that undergirds our faith in all seasons. One final disclaimer: there are many ways to present the colors and the seasons of faith. My goal is simply to show how reclaiming our Christian heritage can help us make sense of our never-ending spiritual journey with Christ.

CHAPTER 1. FROM BLACK AND WHITE TO LIVING COLOR

Two cautions are in order. First, our personal seasons of faith may or may not coincide with the church's calendar. We may be struggling with profound grief (a time of purple anguish) while the church is joyfully celebrating in a white season of all-out gladness. The four colors provide a template for us, but the timing of our individual faith journey is not regulated by calendar dates. Second, the seasons are not a one-time experience for us. We may enter the purple of Advent (waiting for Christ to appear in our daily life) on multiple occasions. The same is true of white and green seasons. There is no once-and-for-all linear progression. Instead, our journey of faith is an ongoing process, surprising us with Christmas white and Pentecost green and the purple of Lent, often in an unpredictable order. For as long as we live the surprises continue.

A COLORFUL FAITH

Teenagers have been known to complain when their parents announce, "We're going to church." Adults can be "down on church" as well. Many would agree with Algernon Charles Swinburne, a 19th-century poet who saw Jesus as the enemy of joy. He wrote: "Thou hast conquered, O pale Galilean; the world has grown grey from thy breath."

But authentic Christianity is not pale or gray. It's not "S.O.P. vanilla."[2] Christians are like Dorothy in *The Wizard of Oz*, carried by a mighty wind into a new world, no longer the black-and-white world of Depression-era Kansas. For Dorothy there was color

---

2 *S.O.P.* is Army talk for Standard Operating Procedure. The phrase "S.O.P. vanilla" comes from a friend at Davidson College, who was making an astute observation: the "same old same old" vanilla ice cream was being served day after day at our fraternity house.

everywhere in Oz: brilliant green (an emerald city), dazzling gold (a yellow brick road), and sparkling red (ruby slippers). For Christians the world becomes equally alive with color. We are led into green pastures by the One who is our shepherd (Psalm 23:2). We are given a rainbow of promise when battered by storms (Genesis 9:8). We believe that God delights in us (Zephaniah 3:17), much as Jacob delighted in Joseph. The coat of many colors that Jacob created is a symbol of unwavering affection (Genesis 37:3).[3]

The entire Bible is a book of colorful stories and colorful people and colorful reminders of God's faithfulness. A crimson cord is tied in Rahab's window to save her and her family (Joshua 2:18). Mordecai wears royal garments of blue and white, along with a purple robe, after the Jews' mortal enemy is hanged on a gallows 75 feet high (Esther 7:9-10, 8:15). In the holy city that comes down from heaven there are jewels of every color, symbols of God's unfailing care (Revelation 21:18-21).

The Bible is no book of sterile platitudes. There are struggles, intrigues, disasters, escapes, and surprises from Genesis to Revelation. Even the genealogies and census reports pique our curiosity. Why are they included in holy scripture? Can we discover something of beauty and worth in Bible verses that seem, at first glance, to be uninspiring and ordinary? The answer, I believe, is an emphatic "Yes!" The "boring" genealogies and census details remind us that God knows each of us. We are not anonymous in the eyes of God.

---

3   We don't know the colors included in the original coat, but in the Broadway musical, *Joseph and the Amazing Technicolor® Dreamcoat*, the palette of colors is stupendous: red and yellow and green and brown and scarlet and black and ocher and peach and ruby and olive and violet and fawn and lilac and gold and chocolate and mauve and cream and crimson and silver and rose and azure and lemon and russet and grey and purple and white and pink and orange and blue!

CHAPTER 1. FROM BLACK AND WHITE TO LIVING COLOR

We misuse the Bible when we reduce it to a list of rules or a set of noble principles. Our spiritual life cannot be defined by simple, dull-gray, one-size-fits-all answers. There is a grandeur and mystery in everyone's story of faith, because each of us—without exception—is a magnificent and unrepeatable creation.

What do we have in common as Christians? We are committed to Christ, our one Lord and Savior. But the roads that lead us to Christ are astonishingly varied. Every story is unique. That is precisely the point of the stories in the Bible, from beginning to end. Yes, there are common themes and similar experiences, but no one's faith story is identical to Abraham's or Hannah's or Timothy's or Priscilla's.

Gideon, for example, is a man who drags his feet in the presence of God. He does his best to escape from God's call, and in doing so, he reminds me of people I know, including myself. Gideon is doubly reluctant. He dares to demand from God a double proof. "I will put a fleece of wool on the threshing floor," he says. "If there is dew on the fleece only, and it is dry on all the ground, then I will know that you will save Israel by my hand" (Judges 6:36-37). But when his demand is met, he insists on a second test: "Can you reverse the conditions, Lord: dry fleece, wet ground?"

Moses is even more hesitant to answer God's call. He presents five creative excuses to the Holy One, insisting that he is not qualified to be a leader. First excuse: Moses protests that he is a nobody. "Who am I, that I should go to Pharaoh?" (Exodus 3:11). Second excuse: Moses fears that the Hebrew people will be spiritually clueless. "Suppose I go to the Israelites and say to them, 'The God of your fathers has sent me to you, and they ask me, 'What is [God's] name?' Then what shall I tell them?' (Exodus 3:13). Third excuse:

Moses resorts to whining. "What if they do not believe me or listen to me?" (Exodus 4:1). Fourth excuse: Moses laments that he is a terrible speaker. How can he presume to address the mightiest ruler on Earth? "O Lord, I have never been eloquent...I am slow of speech and tongue" (Exodus 4:10). The final excuse: Moses digs in his heels and pleads with God. "O Lord, please send someone else to do it" (Exodus 4:13). God's patience with Moses—and with us—is astonishing!

Naomi struggles in a different way. When there is a famine in the land of Israel, she and her husband become exiles in Moab. Her two boys, when old enough to marry, take foreign wives. What else can they do, since there are no other candidates for courtship? Then come the bitterest blows of all. Three blows in succession. Husband, older son, and younger son—they all die. Stunned, unable to imagine that life can be worth living, she sends away (or tries to send away) both of the young women who have married into her family. She assumes her life is over. But God has other plans for Naomi (Ruth 1:1-22).

The stories are rich and varied. Mephibosheth finds a compassionate protector who is the man most hated by his grandfather (II Samuel 9:6-7). A passerby named Simon is minding his own business on a Friday in Jerusalem when he is commanded to join the death march of Jesus. His life and the life of his sons, Alexander and Rufus, are never the same (Mark 15:21). Lydia is a wealthy woman in the Roman Empire, a "seller of purple," who gathers with her friends to search for spiritual truth. When Paul appears at their meeting place one Sabbath day, she takes a bold—perhaps impulsive—step. She invites this stranger into her home and opens not only her spacious quarters but also her

CHAPTER 1. FROM BLACK AND WHITE TO LIVING COLOR

heart and her mind to Paul's message of hope (Acts 16:14-15).

Why is the Bible so strangely diverse? Why doesn't God give us a simple list of rules to follow and forget about the stories? Actually, there *is* a simple list. Jesus reduces the 613 commandments of Moses to two: love for God and love for neighbor (Mark 12:30-31). So why are there hundreds of stories? Why include Micaiah's confrontation with the 400 false prophets (I Kings 22:1-27)? Or Oholiab's immediate yes, when skilled artisans are needed in the desert (Exodus 36:1-2)? Or a woman's tears, as she interrupts a formal banquet and angers Simon the Pharisee (Luke 7:36-38)? The answer is that none of us are clones. Yes, we are called by God to find our way home—that is, to the place where all is well in God's holy presence. But before we arrive at our spiritual home, we must travel a pathway that no one has ever traveled in exactly the same way. Each of us has never-before-created fingerprints. We also have never-before-encountered stories and never-before-lived adventures.

The richness of the Bible suggests that our stories today can be equally complex and intriguing and beautiful and painful and hopeful. If God can bring life and healing from the tangled mess described in the Old and New Testaments, then surely God can meet us on our never-before-traveled pathways. We can learn from the mistakes of those who have gone before us. We can be inspired by their progress. We can affirm that the One who delivered our wise and foolish ancestors can deliver us from whatever we may face in the 21st century.

For the first few years of my life, there was no TV in my home. World War II had ended. TV sets were not yet being produced for mass consumption. Eventually my family was blessed with a tiny-screen, black-and-white contraption that we could see if we pulled our chairs up close. Baseball games were almost impossible to follow on those primitive sets, but "Sky King" and "The $64,000-Dollar Question" and "I Love Lucy" came across quite well. We were content, until one New Year's Day we visited a friend's home to watch the Rose Parade. For the first time in my life the familiar images on the screen were in living color. For the first time I realized: "I've been missing so much!"

As we rediscover the richness of faith stories—in the Bible and in our world today—what may have seemed ordinary and humdrum can come to life for us. We can experience a palette of colors more diverse than the colors in Joseph's dreamcoat. And we can take heart: the colors of faith can guide us, as each of us finds our unique way to arrive safely at home.

THE COLORS OF HEART AND HEAD TOGETHER

A few militant skeptics, like Sam Harris and Richard Dawkins, have become *New York Times* bestselling authors, wielding rhetorical swords and "proving"—to their own satisfaction—that religion is irrational and foolish. At best, they say, it is a waste of time. At worst, they say, it endangers our planet, as dogmatic believers square off against everyone who disagrees with them.

Others who reject religion today are less hostile in their attacks, but they cannot understand the concept of faith. They ask, "How can you believe in an invisible being who answers prayer and forgives sin and conquers death?" Their questions are reasonable. They want to know: "Do you have any evidence that such things are possible? Or are you simply turning off your brain when you go to church?"

We can respond by pointing to the work of Albert Einstein, whose work a century ago reshaped the world of science. (The

CHAPTER 1. FROM BLACK AND WHITE TO LIVING COLOR

year 1914 was an astonishingly creative time for Einstein. Multiple breakthroughs occurred.[4]) Einstein showed that Newton's "immutable" laws do not apply for the entire universe—or even for the planet Earth—with perfect exactness. The laws of nature, in other words, cannot fully explain the mysteries of life.[5]

Other scientists have concurred, especially in the fields of physics, mathematics, medicine, clinical psychology, sociology, and anthropology. Strong evidence has been offered to contradict the black-and-white materialism that once prevailed. Materialism declares: "Nothing is real but space, time, energy, and matter." A more adequate worldview, many now believe, takes seriously two kinds of reality: (1) physical reality, known through sense experience and reason; and (2) non-physical reality, known in many ways, including dreams, religious ritual, and meditation. Groundbreaking works by Jerome Frank (*Persuasion and Healing*), Elisabeth Kubler-Ross (*On Life after Death, Revised*), C. G. Jung (*Memories, Dreams, Reflections*), Morton Kelsey (*Afterlife*), and others have helped make this view credible. Both the physical realm and the non-physical realm can be studied and affirmed in responsible ways.

If I have a materialistic worldview, if I am the accidental product of a blind chain of events that began 4.5 billion years ago, when the Earth came into being, or 14 billion years ago, when the Big Bang set everything into motion, then nothing is permanent. Nothing is of enduring value. I am part of a flux that has no ultimate purpose. Is that my story? Is everything simply a blur,

---

4   See Walter Isaacson, *Einstein: His Life and Universe* (New York: Simon and Schuster, 2008).

5   For a more thorough discussion of Einstein's work and its implications for religious faith, see Morton Kelsey, *Encounter with God* (Minneapolis: Bethany House, 1972).

flickering into existence only to be extinguished forever? "It is terrible," writes militant atheist Sam Harris, "that we all die and lose everything we love" (*Letter to a Christian Nation*, p. 56).

What is the color of such hopelessness? At times it is black and white, claiming with absolute certainty that "my way is the only way" and that there is no such thing as non-physical reality. At other times this view can be represented by the color gray. Is there no ultimate purpose in the universe? Then the future is gray and bleak indeed.

But what if our worldview allows for two equally significant realities? What if we begin to affirm—with intellectual integrity—that there is a spiritual realm that coexists with the physical world of space/time/energy/matter? There is then a purpose, a destiny, a goal toward which we are traveling. Our journey is not a senseless joke. Paul points to a future of brilliant and enduring color, when he says: "I consider that our present sufferings are not worth comparing with the glory that will be revealed in us" (Romans 8:18). C. S. Lewis says it especially well for me when he describes in *The Chronicles of Narnia* the realm of the spirit: "And they went through winding valley after winding valley... till at last at the end of one long lake which looked as blue as a turquoise, they saw a smooth green hill. Its sides were as steep as the sides of a pyramid and round the very top of it ran a great wall; but above the wall rose the branches of trees whose leaves looked like silver and their fruit like gold" (*The Last Battle*, p. 219). This is symbolic language, of course, but it points toward a reality that is in no way dull or drab.

Lewis goes on to say that we are surrounded by every imaginable gift of beauty and dazzling color, but some of us are blind. Not

CHAPTER 1. FROM BLACK AND WHITE TO LIVING COLOR

because we are being punished by a wrathful deity, but because we are sitting in paradise with our eyes closed. We have the innate ability to see, but we haven't learned to live with open eyes, open minds, and open hearts.[6]

My hope is that *The Colors of Faith* can help us see the goodness of God in living color. If we are willing to explore with our minds and listen with our hearts, we can delight in our journey of faith. From purple. Through white. To green. By means of red.

---

6 John's gospel makes a similar point in chapter 3, verse 19: "This is the verdict: Light has come into the world, but people loved darkness instead of light."

QUESTIONS FOR DISCUSSION

1. Have there been times in your life when religion seemed boring to you? When, if ever, did it begin to change from dull gray to living color?

2. Are you surprised by the candor of the Bible? Many so-called heroes are far from perfect. There is squalor as well as beauty. Why do you think this holiest of books for Christians and Jews is so shockingly human? Would you prefer a "cleaned up" book of Scripture, without so much human messiness?

3. Is it possible for intelligent, well-educated Christians to believe in life after death? Or is faith a matter of simply believing, not asking questions, "turning off one's brain"?

Chapter 2. PURPLE

Purple is the color of confusion and pain. The sadness begins in Genesis, chapter 3, when the entire creation becomes damaged and flawed.[7] As people of faith, we never forget that life has a tragic dimension.

Where does my personal journey of faith begin? With purple. No matter how much success I enjoy, there are disappointments and struggles. I wish I could undo my mistakes. I wish I could find more joy in the daily grind. I'm waiting for something that I desperately need, but what is it? I can't quite say.

We call it the season of Advent. A purple time of waiting in the dark. Hoping. Longing. Wishing. But will it happen? Maybe, we

---

[7] In the first chapter of Genesis there is a joyful refrain: "And God saw that it was good" (Gen 1:10, 12, 18, 21, 25). When the work of creation is finished, the affirmation is even more emphatic: "God saw everything that he had made, and indeed, it was very good" (Gen 1:31). Genesis 2 continues the description of paradise on Earth. Then comes Genesis 3, the first of many painful stories, stories of disobedience, deceit, and disaster. Violence follows in Genesis 4, when Cain murders Abel, and a downward spiral of evil is underway. Finally, we are told, in one of the most poignant passages in all of Scripture: "The Lord saw that the wickedness of humankind was great in the earth, and that every inclination of the thoughts of their hearts was only evil continually. And the Lord was very sorry that he had made humankind on the earth, and it grieved him to his heart" (Gen 6:5-6). But God is gracious, deciding to continue the human experiment with Noah and Noah's family. How does Noah respond? Delivered from the flood, Noah begins his new life by drinking himself into a stupor (Gen 9:20-21).

say. But deep down we sense that life is not a fairy tale. We will not live happily ever after. Or will we?

There is a second purple season in the church. Even when Jesus was here with us, he was betrayed and abandoned. The purple season of Lent confronts us with the pain of his crucifixion and death—and our own failures and unavoidable death.

Both purple experiences are essential for us in the church: one before the Christmas surprise ("Do not be afraid…to you is born this day in the city of David a Savior, who is the Messiah, the Lord"[8]) and one before the Easter surprise ("Do not be afraid; I know that you are looking for Jesus who was crucified. He is not here; for he has been raised, as he said"[9]). Unfortunately, we are tempted to emphasize the joyful surprises and ignore the grim realities that precede the good news. In recent years blue has become a popular substitute for purple on the four Advent Sundays before December 25, an almost-too-pretty blue for an almost-too-pretty season.[10] It's as if we want to hide from the ugliness in our world, skipping over anything that reminds us of human suffering. C. S. Lewis describes Narnia before the Aslan's arrival as endlessly dreary, a place where it is always winter and never Christmas. We seem to prefer a world where it is always Christmas and never winter. "Don't spoil the month of December," some church members say, "with reminders of human poverty and human pain. Don't talk about anything dark

---

8   Luke 2:10–11.

9   Matthew 28:5–6.

10 Blue can be appropriate during Advent, if we are careful to remember that blue is a slightly less dark substitute for the darkness of purple. Those who are cynical may argue that the blue of Advent was separated from the purple of Lent for commercial reasons: by adding a new color to the Christian calendar, sellers of church paraments and clergy stoles could increase their profits.

CHAPTER 2. PURPLE

when there is a lovely crèche on the altar of our church." In other words, let's get rid of the distressing purple of Advent.

It's much harder to deny the pain during Lent. Lent is forty days of walking with Jesus toward Golgotha, the Place of the Skull. There is no way to make Holy Week—and the five Sundays preceding Holy Week—pretty. But we are tempted to trivialize the season of Lent. "I'm giving up chocolate (or soap operas or video games) for Lent" can be a substitute for honest self-examination, the kind of self-searching that leads to earnest prayer, as in Psalm 51: "Create in me a clean heart, O God, and put a new and right spirit within me" (v. 10). We will never be clean unless we look at the problem areas that cause us grief: grudges, addictions,[11] disappointments, loneliness. But because it's never pleasant to face our personal demons, we often focus on what is less demanding.

The bottom line is this: purple reminds us of our need for God. The message that "all have sinned and fall short of the glory of God" (Romans 3:23) has never been popular. But unless we are willing to "do purple," unless we are willing to admit that our life without God has become unmanageable,[12] we will fall short of the glory that can be ours.

---

[11] Addictions are not limited to substance addictions such as alcohol, drugs, or food. Process addictions (such as sex and gambling) can be equally enslaving.

[12] Recovering alcoholics begin with the Step One of the Twelve Steps: "We admitted we were powerless over alcohol—that our lives had become unmanageable." This is an equally important first step for non-alcoholics: "We admitted we were powerless over sinful attitudes and habits …"

There is an old gospel song that declares "The way of the cross leads home."[13] Have we forgotten the good news—and the warning—that comes to us through the color purple? The sadness of the cross, the sadness of purple, is the pathway that brings us home to God. When we try to avoid the dark seasons of the Christian life, we remain shallow and self-absorbed. Can we acknowledge our brokenness? Can we admit our need for God's healing and grace?

A. PURPLE EVERYWHERE: "SOMETHING'S WRONG"

A familiar hymn asks each of us: "Have we trials and temptations? Is there trouble anywhere?"[14] The answer is "Yes! A thousand times yes!"

Trials?
- A young man goes off to war, confident and idealistic. He returns home, having seen the face of hell, with PTSD and a permanent loss of innocence.
- A woman who has attended church faithfully for 80 years finds herself in a nursing home, no longer continent, no longer able to see because of macular degeneration.
- A teenager learns that her parents are moving toward a bitter divorce.
- A young boy is gifted artistically but struggles with math and reading. Every school day is a never-ending struggle.

---

13 "The Way of the Cross Leads Home," lyrics by Jesse Brown Pound, music by Charles H. Gabriel.
14 "What a Friend We Have in Jesus," lyrics by Joseph M. Scriven, music by Charles C. Converse.

CHAPTER 2. PURPLE

Temptations?
- A married man becomes obsessed with a woman he meets while traveling.
- A retired teacher feels obsolete, no longer needed or valued. She withdraws into a world of loneliness.
- A college student finds it easy to do the minimum amount of work instead of studying each day.
- A bright young adult is seduced by flattering words and the promise of big money as he interviews for a job that does not connect with his true self.

Is there trouble anywhere? If we read the daily news, we know that our world is broken. Yes, there is extraordinary beauty everywhere in God's world. But tremendous beauty, when spoiled or damaged or degraded, makes for devastating tragedy. There is graphic horror at times, as when a U.S. Army veteran opens fire on peaceful worshipers in Wisconsin, worshipers who wear turbans and therefore seem disturbing to the tragically deranged shooter. There are ever-present global problems as well, problems of poverty and malnutrition and disease that blight the lives of innocent children. But the trouble in our world is in no way limited to headline stories or global issues. There are daily troubles in the daily lives of almost everyone we know. It may be a bout of lower back pain. Or a fellow employee who annoys everyone with her constant complaining. Or a shrinking checkbook balance. Or a careless driver who causes a minor accident. Or a son who forgets his mother's birthday—again. Or an unpleasant number on the bathroom scale. Or children who fight every day over who gets to use the computer. Or a broken furnace in January. Or a phone call from the emergency room after midnight.

The bad news is undeniable: something is wrong with our world. The Buddha, in his First Noble Truth, taught that the suffering of birth, old age, sickness, and death is unavoidable. Christians have a different understanding of tragedy—we believe that human sin is ultimately to blame—but we agree that no one is exempt from suffering. The sadness of the color purple will always be with us.

What does purple feel like? It is heavy and disheartening. In purple seasons we are restless and unfulfilled. We long for something that we desperately want, but what would satisfy us? Would winning the Power Ball lottery make us happy forever? Not really. What if we were supremely attractive and popular? Would we be perfectly content? Not for long. Would more sex or better sex or unlimited sex make all our dreams come true? Not a chance. If we could live for a thousand years and not be ravaged by time, would that be enough for us? No, we need something more than mere existence.

But there is good news. The purple feeling that drags us down can be our greatest blessing, if it nudges us toward a life-changing moment, a moment when we discover: "Truly my soul finds rest in God" (Psalm 62:1). Do I have a great need for God? If the answer is yes, I can discover God's unfailing love.

And so the color purple is essential for followers of Jesus. It stirs in us a yearning for more than daily struggles. It reminds us that honest suffering and desperate need are the pathway to a life that is productive and blessed.

B. PURPLE SEASONS IN THE CHURCH

When Christians read the Old Testament, we see good news and bad news. God promises a homeland for the family of Abraham

CHAPTER 2. PURPLE

and Sarah—very good news. But when that family is established in a "land flowing with milk and honey" (Deuteronomy 31:20), they struggle. Even before they arrive in Canaan, they turn away from God, complaining in the wilderness, worshiping a golden calf, preferring slavery in Egypt to freedom with Moses.[15]

Despite the best intentions of countless men and women in the Bible, there is a power of evil, a dark side, that afflicts us all of us. Again and again God promises spiritual health and well-being, if only we will trust and obey. But instead of trusting the One who has been faithful in the past, we complain about our daily hardships. We whine about the challenges that are before us. We fall into spiritual darkness.

"I want to do what is honorable and right," we say. And we mean it. We want to be faithful. But our hearts are wayward. Sooner or later we find ourselves dabbling in the sins of:

- Pride. "I thank you, Lord, that I am not like my neighbor."
- Envy. "It's not fair. My neighbor has more than I do."
- Anger. "I'll get even with my annoying neighbor."
- Sloth. "Being a good neighbor is hard work. Why bother?"
- Gluttony. "Come on, neighbor. Let's eat, drink, and be merry."
- Greed. "So what if my neighbor doesn't have enough? I want more for myself."
- Lust. "I want to consume you, neighbor, in the name of love."

---

15 The complaining is constant. See, for example, Exodus 14:11, Exodus 17:3, and Numbers 21:5.

Are these minor failings? Or is there wisdom in our Judeo-Christian tradition, which insists that they are deadly sins? We are told through the prophet Jeremiah: "Your pain is incurable. Because your guilt is great, because your sins are so numerous, I have done these things to you [sending the punishment of a merciless foe]" (Jeremiah 30:14–15).

Is willpower the answer? Can we clean up our act by trying harder? Will our religious practices cleanse us and make us pure? No, we are told in Hebrew and Christian Scripture.[16] Human effort can treat the symptoms, but the underlying illness—a wayward heart, a restless spirit—remains.

This is bad news for many of us. I remember my early days in Sunday School, when I was terribly confused by the Old Testament. No matter what Moses did to threaten or cajole the people of Israel, they kept disobeying God. "What's wrong with those people?" I kept asking. "Why don't they learn? Why don't they straighten up and fly right?" I was too young to understand the subtle self-deceit that we are all capable of.

Fast forward 55 years. I was attending a public service of remembrance in Tucson, Arizona, along with thousands of my fellow Tucsonans. We were gathered on January 8, 2012, the first anniversary of the shooting attack on Congresswoman Gabrielle Giffords and innocent bystanders. Nineteen Tucsonans had been shot at point-blank range; six had died. We were still grieving, as we honored the memory of the victims and as we prayed for our community

---

16 See Psalm 51:16–17, Jeremiah 17:9, Micah 6:6–8, Romans 7:21–24, Hebrews 7:27–28. Religion at its best is waiting for God, attending to God, learning to receive the gifts of God. It is not a way of bargaining with God. It is not a tit-for-tat transaction, as if to say: "I'll do this for you, Lord; now you owe me."

CHAPTER 2. PURPLE

and nation. The evening was cold. I was shivering as the Tucson Symphony Orchestra called us together with solemn music. There were speeches, profound reflections offered by community leaders.[17] Gabby Giffords herself led all of us in the Pledge of Allegiance. But what touched me most deeply was a familiar hymn from the Christian tradition. The words were modified slightly by inserting a refrain after every verse, a refrain that expressed our enduring sorrow, a refrain that pointed to the darkness within each of us. The Tucson Symphony Chorus sang these haunting words: "Prone to wander, Lord, I feel it; prone to leave the God I love. Here's my heart, O take and seal it; seal it for thy courts above."[18] Instead of lashing out at the perpetrator of this horrifying tragedy, we were confessing that we ourselves have wayward hearts. Most of us have not committed acts of physical violence. But we are not perfectly innocent or pure.

The bombed-out ruins of the cathedral in Coventry, England, declare the same truth. The rubble of stones and timbers, destroyed in Nazi bombing raids, has never been cleared away. Under an open sky, the collapsed cathedral walls are a grim reminder of World War II. Where the high altar once stood there are two pieces of burned and blackened wood, placed together to form a cross. Beneath the cross are two words: "Father, forgive." Not "Father, forgive them…" But simply, "Father, forgive." All of us need God's mercy. No one is fully righteous in God's eyes. As people of faith, we cannot tell our story unless we begin with the color purple.

---

17 Speakers included Mark Kelly, Congresswoman Giffords' husband; Eugene Sander, President of the University of Arizona; Ken Bennett, Arizona Secretary of State; Jonathan Rothschild, Mayor of Tucson; Dr. Peter Rhee, Chief of the University Medical Center's Division of Trauma, Critical Care and Emergency Surgery; and Rabbi Stephanie Aaron, Congregation Chaverim.

18 "Come, Thou Fount of Every Blessing," lyrics by Robert Robinson, music by John Wyeth.

ADVENT

Advent is purple because the Prince of Peace has not fully arrived. We are still waiting for the King of Love. "All Earth is waiting," we sing during Advent.[19] Waiting can be agony.

In Samuel Beckett's classic stage play, *Waiting for Godot*, the long-expected one remains absent from beginning to end. The message seems to be: "Don't get your hopes up; he's not coming." Christians have already welcomed the Savior of the world—"Joy to the world! The Lord is come!"—but we are waiting still. Our dreams of lasting peace are not fully realized. We continue to hope for a compassionate world where every child is deeply valued, but millions remain unloved.

"How long, O Lord?" is the cry of psalmists and prophets.[20] "How long must we wait for your will to be done on Earth as it is in heaven?" The disciples of Jesus are asking a similar question 40 days after Easter: "Lord, is this the time when you will restore the kingdom to Israel?" (Acts 1:6). They are saying, even when the Risen Christ is with them: "The world is not as it should be. Something is wrong."

And so we begin the Christian year with purple. The four purple Sundays of Advent are a time every year:

1. To remember the centuries before Christ was born, centuries of disappointment and longing.
2. To reflect on the brokenness in our world today, a world not fully healed, a world of continuing sin and sadness.

---

19 "All Earth Is Waiting (Toda la Tierra)," lyrics and music by Alberto Taulé.
20 See, for example: Psalm 13:1-2, Psalm 35:17, Psalm 89:46, Isaiah 6:11, Habakkuk 1:2, Revelation 6:10.

CHAPTER 2. PURPLE

No purple would mean no honesty about human sorrow. No purple would be a denial of human suffering, the kind of suffering we saw during World War II, when more than 50 million human beings perished. We have also seen quiet suffering, as in families where no one seems to listen and no one seems to care.

"Come, Lord Jesus" is our cry during Advent. "Come and save us from ourselves. Come and convince us that peace is possible, that politicians with opposing views can work together for the common good, that spouses who are anxious and estranged can learn to love again, that feared strangers can become valued neighbors."

We have an incredibly difficult journey ahead of us. We are Muslims and Christians, gays and straights, rich and poor, hardliners and moderates, Anglos and Latinos. How can we possibly build bridges of mutual respect and understanding? Advent does not promise easy solutions. There are tears to be shed, as we confront our failures. There is pain to be experienced, as we acknowledge again and again that the world is broken. Why are children abandoned? Why are children abused? Why are children undernourished? Why are children left behind in underperforming schools?

During Advent we long for a new heaven and a new earth. We need a Savior, a Savior who has come to us in the past and who is coming again. He is already with us, but he has not yet completed his work. We are recalcitrant. We are slow of heart to believe.[21] We pray for the coming of Christ, only to hesitate, wondering if he will actually appear. And so the question remains: "Is healing possible, or will we be purple forever?"

---

21 The Risen Christ speaks these words on the very day of Easter, as he walks with two disciples toward Emmaus. "Oh, how foolish you are, and how slow of heart to believe ..." (Luke 24:25).

LENT

Lent is also purple, beginning on Ash Wednesday and continuing through Holy Week. Lent reminds us that even when we know God's love in Jesus, we are not home-free. We are still self-absorbed at times, stuck in our old patterns of envy, anger, lust, greed, sloth, gluttony, and pride. "Wretched man that I am!" Paul cries out, *after* he becomes a follower of Christ. "Who will rescue me from this body of death?" (Romans 7:24).

The original disciples, 12 in number, were privileged to see Jesus daily. They traveled with him. They loved him enough to leave everything else—home, family, and work (Matthew 19:27). But in the hour of his greatest need, they abandoned him.[22] The problem was not Judas alone. Peter also failed, as did Andrew and John and Matthew and all of his closest friends.

If we are tempted today to feel overconfident as people of faith, the season of Lent brings us down into the dust. "Lord, have mercy" is not a one-time prayer, when we are deciding for the first time to follow Jesus. We are always confessing our weakness as disciples, even after years of faithful service.

This is the paradox that non-believers cannot grasp: "When I am weak, then I am strong" (II Corinthians 12:10). When I recognize my own frailty, God is able to lift me up and empower me. But as long as I insist that I am capable of doing great things for God in my own strength, I am nothing more than a noisy gong or a

---

[22] Mark 14:50 is a verse that can shake us to the core. Mark tells us that "they *all* forsook him and fled" (emphasis added).

clanging symbol,[23] a human pretender puffing up my chest, strutting about as if I were divine. "No!" says the color purple. The way to life is not to stand up in church and give a glowing testimony, boasting that "Before I knew Christ I was a terrible so-and-so, but now that I'm saved I'm the nicest person you could ever hope to meet." The *only* way to live abundantly and eternally is to repent in dust and ashes—again and again—confessing: "I need thee every hour, most gracious Lord."[24]

The purple of Lent calls us to permanent humility. The word "humility" can be traced to the Indo-European root word *ghôm*, best translated by the English word "humus." That is where our spiritual journey begins: on our knees in the humus, in dust and ashes . Even when we have done our best, we confess our need for God's healing and forgiveness.

C. PURPLE SEASONS IN ME

ADVENT. I lived in the purple season of Advent until I was 13 years old.[25] Even though I attended church with my family, enjoying Sunday School and worship (the songs were lively), Vacation Bible School (the games were fun), and family night suppers (unlimited desserts), I had not a clue that Christ could be a living presence in my life. I had never listened to a sermon from start to finish. I

---

[23] When Paul says that without love "I am a noisy gong or a clanging cymbal" (I Corinthians 13:1), he is talking about the love of Christ. Without the *agape* love of Christ, our most exalted speech is mere noise. Paul is making the same point that Jesus made in the Upper Room: "Apart from me you can do nothing" (John 15:5).

[24] "I Need Thee Every Hour," lyrics by Annie S. Hawks, music by Robert Lowry.

[25] Advent in my life was not a one-time experience. There have been a number of Advent-like seasons for me, when it was difficult to perceive Christ's presence in our world. I am describing here my first Advent, before I knew Christ in a personal and life-changing way.

used the preaching time to fold church bulletins into paper airplanes. Did I need a deeper relationship with God? "Not really," I would have said during those Advent years. My life was just fine, I thought. Yes, I was often in trouble at school for talking in class and being disruptive. "So what?" I told myself. "I'm a normal kid."

I was oblivious to God's love, and so it was Advent for me, a purple season of incompleteness. I didn't know that I was waiting for Christmas—not Christmas on the calendar, but Christmas as a life-changing encounter with the God of amazing grace.

LENT. Like every follower of Christ, I have failed at times. Some of my failures have been short-lived, minor mistakes: forgetting an appointment, losing my temper while driving. Minor failures are common for all of us. They give us a brief glimpse of purple, a brief reminder that we are human and fallible.

But every now and then we feel devastated by the sin of the world and by our own inadequacy. One of those painful seasons in my life lasted for two and a half years. A colleague had abused a number of women in our church, and I was left to clean up the mess. Some of the women felt that I was not as helpful as I should have been, and their criticism was quite harsh. It became uglier and uglier, and the pain was not easily healed. Could I have been a better pastor for the victims? Yes. I had good intentions, but even as I tried to help, I was not succeeding. It was a dark night of the soul for me and for many others.

We should not be surprised when we find ourselves in the purple season of Lent. No one is exempt from sorrow. No one is always wise and 100 percent righteous. And so we continue to pray, as long as we live: "Have mercy on me, O God, according to your steadfast love; according to your abundant mercy blot out my transgressions" (Psalm 51:1).

D. THEOLOGY IN THE COLOR PURPLE

THE PURPLE DILEMMA
Christian theology begins with the goodness of God and the goodness of God's creation. But in the next breath theologians add: "Something went wrong." The Bible calls it sin. Through the centuries we have called it original sin, an often confusing term. It simply means that once sin appeared in the universe, it was pervasive.[26] Just as a drop of ink in a glass of clear water stains all of the water, our human sinfulness unleashes a perversity that affects everything that God has made.

Karl Menninger's best-selling book of the 1980s, *Whatever Became of Sin?*, argues that the unpopular word "sin" can be an ennobling concept. If we are sinful, then we are responsible for our thoughts and our behavior. No sin means no responsibility, no ability to shape our destiny, no human freedom or dignity. There is a problem, however. If we are free to make choices, why do we continue to abuse that freedom? Why do *all* of us fall into sin? Is sin inevitable? If so, how can we claim to be free? It has always been a baffling question.

On the one hand, we are responsible and free. On the other hand, sin is present in every human life, no matter how righteous

---

[26] Even in those who appear most proper and most righteous—"practically perfect in every way"—there are improper desires and secret shames. The New Testament reaffirms the obvious: "If we say that we have no sin, we deceive ourselves, and the truth is not in us" (I John 1:8).

we try to be. Albert Outler, the much-admired Wesley scholar, wrestles with this dilemma in his 1975 book *Theology in the Wesleyan Spirit*.[27] He concludes that God does not compel us to abuse our freedom or to deny our radical dependence as finite creatures. But we constantly rebel against our limitations. We want to be godlike so that all of our dreams can come true. We want to enjoy the fruit of the forbidden tree, reserved for God alone (Genesis 3:1-5). This universal rebellion is our original sin.

Theology in the color purple can be summarized using the acronym CUP—IF.[28]

C = **Chronic**
Our sin is a permanent condition like diabetes. It is not like a temporary bout of the flu.

U = **Universal**
No one is exempt. No one can claim to be sinless.

P = **Progressive**
Just as one falsehood leads to other falsehoods, one sin leads to sinful habits and patterns that are pervasive.

I = **Incurable**
There is no human remedy for our sin. Moralistic strategies are doomed to fail.

F = **Fatal**
This is no minor illness. Sin will eventually destroy us, along with our planet.

---

27 Albert C. Outler, *Theology in the Wesleyan Spirit* (Nashville: Discipleship Resources, 1975).

28 We must drink from Jesus' "CUP—IF" we want to live. This is what Jesus told his disciples when they were bickering and jostling for prestige (Matthew 20:22).

CHAPTER 2. PURPLE

The seriousness of human sin was a key insight of the Protestant Reformation. We cannot clean up our act by contributing money, no matter how large the amount. We cannot climb to heaven on a ladder of virtue. Our only hope is for God to "come down" to us.

Sin is like quicksand. The more we struggle to extract ourselves from the inescapable mire, the more stuck we become. Like the addictions that we know so well in the 21st century—addictions that range from alcoholism to workaholism, from eating disorders to people pleasing and codependence—sin is cunning and baffling, ensnaring us when we are overconfident, reminding us again and again that "I do not do the good I want, but the evil I do not want is what I do" (Romans 7:19).

What can we do if we are stuck in a purple morass? If sin is a tragic, incurable illness, is there hope for us—realistic hope, not wishful thinking? The answer for Christians has always been bad news and good news. The bad news is: "Apart from me you can do nothing" (John 15:5). But at the same time: "With God all things are possible" (Matthew 19:26).

GOD'S GIFT WHEN THE WORLD IS PURPLE
John Wesley's theology begins with the grace of God, God's willingness to love us when we are spiritually hostile or spiritually asleep. Some of us are indeed hostile, consciously rebelling against our Creator. But many of us are simply unaware of God's goodness and mercy. It is as if we are sleepwalking through life, failing to notice the miracle of God's world. We are like the Webb family in Thornton Wilder's *Our Town*. Emily Webb has been dead for 14 years. As she looks back from her new life beyond death, her greatest desire is to re-experience one of her happiest days in the

past. "I want to revisit my 12th birthday," she decides. When her wish is granted, she is painfully disappointed. She cries out (even though no one can hear her): "Oh, Mama, just look at me one minute as though you really saw me…Let's look at one another."[29] As she returns to the cemetery, she says a final good bye: "Good-by, world. Good-by, Grover's Corners…Mama and Papa. Good-by to clocks ticking…and Mama's sunflowers. And food and coffee. And new-ironed dresses and hot baths…and sleeping and waking up. Oh, earth, you're too wonderful for anybody to realize you. Do any human beings ever realize life while they live it?—every, every minute?"[30]

Prevenient grace is God's response to our dullness and to every form of spiritual darkness. Whether we are ignoring God or actively rebelling against God, we are missing the joy that could be ours. How can we find our way to a new life of joy and abundance? The secret is prevenient grace. (*Pre* means "before." *Venient* means "to come.") Prevenient grace comes *before* we are awake. God cares for us *before* we care about God. God pokes us and prods us and makes us restless long *before* we realize who is pursuing us.

"Listen! I am standing at the door, knocking; if you hear my voice and open the door, I will come in to you and eat with you, and you with me" (Revelation 3:20). The Risen Christ speaks these words, pleading with us to pay attention to that restless feeling that we so often ignore. "Isn't there more to life?" we wonder. "What am I missing?"

---

29 Thornton Wilder, *Our Town* (New York: Coward-McCann, 1939), p. 107.
30 *Ibid.*, p. 108.

CHAPTER 2. PURPLE

We resist the Holy One for a hundred reasons. "I don't want to be a religious fanatic," we say. Or: "My life is not so bad. I don't want to take the risk of changing." Or: "Religion is for losers." Or: "There's no proof that God is real." Or: "If I believe in God, my freedom will be restricted." Or: "Religion is boring." Or: "I wish I could believe it, but Christianity is like a fairy tale." Or: "The church is full of hypocrites."

But God's grace pursues us through the years, finding small ways—or sometimes dramatic ways—to say "Wake up!" God's grace keeps knocking at the door, tapping gently most of the time. It is a love that will not leave us alone. "I love you this much," says the Creator of the universe, stretching out arms of love on the cross.[31] Before we ever dreamed that we could know the healing, cleansing, empowering, life-changing love of God, God was working in subtle, often imperceptible, ways to lead us from our purple haze into a new life of brilliant beauty. Thanks to prevenient grace, there is hope for all of us.

OUR RESPONSE TO PREVENIENT GRACE

Denial is our most familiar response. When we receive a wake-up call from God, or repeated wake-up calls, we tend to do nothing at all. Few of us enjoy going to the doctor when we sense that something is wrong: "What if the doctor has bad news for me? What if the doctor tells me that I have a chronic, progressive illness that is incurable and fatal?" And so we procrastinate. We fail to confront the painful truth, preferring to live in ignorance.

---

[31] This is Paul's message in Romans 5:8: "While we still were sinners Christ died for us." God's love for us begins before we are awake and aware.

But if the pain is great enough, or if the possibility of healing is credible enough, we may pray the famous prayer of Simon Peter, one of the shortest and most powerful prayers ever uttered: "Lord, save me" (Matthew 14:30). Peter was desperate enough to cry out to Jesus, as he was going under, drowning in the Sea of Galilee. Jesus reached out his hand and caught him, pulling him to safety. The same gift can be ours.

We are hesitant for many reasons. When we stand before Jesus, the Great Physician, we see the full extent of our spiritual sickness. We realize, more clearly than ever before, that "we have left undone those things which we ought to have done, and we have done those things which we ought not to have done."[32]

But there is good news. We can discover that **repentance** is the doorway into God's loving presence. If we can humbly confess our need for God, crying out for help when we are in danger of drowning, we can find God's power and God's peace.

There is a church in Bethlehem, built over the traditional site of the manger. But the Church of the Nativity, as it is known, is unique in all the world. There is only one door into the building, a small door that cannot be entered without bending low. There was once a practical reason for making the sanctuary so difficult to approach, a reason that dates back to armed conflict between enemies. If the only doorway was small, attackers on horseback could not strike down the worshipers inside. Today, however, the diminished-in-size entranceway has a different purpose. It tells us how to be spiritually healthy. The secret is this: to approach the

---

32 *The United Methodist Hymnal*, 891.

CHAPTER 2. PURPLE

manger and leave behind our old life of sadness and self-will, we must bend low. We must bow in humility, admitting to God and to ourselves that we are powerless over sin and that our lives have become unmanageable. Like Peter, we can be rescued—but only if we cry out, repenting of our determination to "do it myself."

Denial is the path of least resistance, the easy way. Repentance is more difficult, but it is the doorway to new life. It brings us from purple sadness into the all-gracious presence of the One whose name is Love.

QUESTIONS FOR DISCUSSION

1. Why is it so difficult for us to be honest about our struggles? Why do we try so hard to convince ourselves (and others) that "Everything is O.K."?

2. How can the purple seasons of Advent and Lent become more meaningful for us, not ignored or trivialized?

3. Is it possible to talk about "deadly sins" and "original sin" in today's world? Can those ancient theological terms be reclaimed in a way that makes sense to people who are thoughtful and intelligent?

4. Have you ever experienced a dark night of the soul? What can we do in times of purple to remain spiritually alive?

Chapter 3. WHITE

White is the color of joy and new beginnings. Not temporary happiness, but lasting joy. We discover that God is real and that God's love enfolds us for all eternity. The purple days are behind us, at least for now. It's time to celebrate.

In the world of ordinary life there are ups and downs. The ups are seldom spectacular: "My son enjoyed his lunch today." The downs seem to be always present: "My son needs braces for his teeth, an unexpected expense of $7,000." Sometimes there are days of spectacular gladness, but there are also days of heartbreak and tragedy. A happy ending is not guaranteed.

But in the church of Jesus we are invited to move from the sadness of purple to the joy that only God can give, the joy of white.[33] We need not remain forever in the darkness of Advent. In spite of

---

[33] White is not like other colors. When white light is passed through a prism, all the colors—from red to violet—are revealed. Nor does white as a liturgical color have racial significance. It's true that some churches have removed "white language" from hymns and prayers. For example, in the hymn "Have Thine Own Way, Lord," the words have been modified for United Methodists. The original text was "Whiter than snow, Lord, wash me just now." The 1989 text omits the first phrase and simply repeats the key idea: "Wash me just now, Lord; wash me just now." Something is lost in poetic imagery, but much is gained in racial sensitivity. In any case, liturgical white has been used without controversy for centuries—the color that is a combination of all colors—to represent what the Bible calls a "joy unspeakable and full of glory" (I Peter 1:8).

our struggles, Christmas comes "to poor ord'n'ry people like you and like I."[34] And when we are most painfully aware of our sins and shortcomings during the purple days of Lent, Easter arrives, as glad and fresh and astonishing as ever, stirring us to "sing with all the saints in glory."[35]

There are two seasons of white for us every year, without fail. Christmas always breaks forth with the light of heaven on December 25. Easter always dawns 46 days after Ash Wednesday,[36] calling us to serve a risen Savior. Both seasons are equally joyful. Both are equally significant for us as Christians. And we do well, for the most part, when it comes to celebrating in the church. Even the most unemotional church attenders are likely to be touched—if only for an instant—by the beauty of poinsettias and candlelight on Christmas Eve. And Easter morning is never a ho-hum day in churches across the entire planet. The message of "He is born!" and "He is risen!" isn't always believed. But the message is alluring nonetheless. Millions hear the good news and are refreshed and renewed. Millions more long for the message of Christmas and Easter to be true, even when they remain skeptical.

For those who say yes to the good news, the white seasons offer hope—hope for our personal raggedness and hope for our beleaguered planet. The message of Christmas has always been "Glory to God in the highest heaven, and on earth peace …" (Luke 2:14). The message of Easter has always been: "Because I live, you also

---

[34] "I Wonder as I Wander," lyrics and music by John Jacob Niles.
[35] "Sing With All the Saints in Glory," lyrics by William J. Irons, music by Ludwig van Beethoven.
[36] The season of Lent is officially 40 weekdays. When the six Sundays of Lent are added, the total is 46 calendar days.

CHAPTER 3. WHITE

will live" (John 14:19). These are not empty words. They announce what is most essential for us as people of faith.

Christmas declares that Jesus is Emmanuel, God *with* us (Matthew 1:23). Easter declares that Jesus is alive today, so that we can know Christ *in* us, the hope of glory (Colossians 1:27). If God is with us, we are comforted; we are not alone. If Christ is in us, we are empowered by the One "who is able to accomplish abundantly far more than all we can ask or imagine" (Ephesians 3:20).

The color white tells us boldly and unequivocally: "Yes, you have a great need for God, and you also have a great God for your need. Your deepest longings can be satisfied. Your brokenness can be healed. Your failures in the past can be forgiven."

Some of us do well with the color purple, acknowledging that we are weary and worn, sin-sick and anxious. Can we do equally well with the color white? Can we allow ourselves to experience the joy that God offers to each of us? God promises that every tear shall be wiped from our eyes and death shall be no more (Revelation 21:4). Can we believe the promise?

A. THE TURNING POINT SEASONS

My favorite baseball player of all time is Ron Santo, Hall of Fame third baseman for the Chicago Cubs.[37] Santo was not only an extraordinary player (a .277 lifetime batting average, 342 home runs, five Gold Gloves, all accomplished while struggling with Type 1 diabetes). He was also a remarkable humanitarian who raised

---

37 The Cubs are often known as the loveable losers of baseball, but it was not always that way. They won two World Series in a row—in 1907 and 1908! And then in 2016 they won the championship again, after only 108 years.

$60,000,000 for the Juvenile Diabetes Research Foundation.[38] But there is another reason why I loved and admired Ronald Edward Santo. He was a passionate and loyal fan, elated when the Cubs played well, crushed when they played poorly. As a radio broadcaster on WGN 720 in Chicago, he expressed exactly what I was feeling at the moment—the anguish ("Oh no!") and the undying hope that every true fan clings to. Late in the season, if the Cubs were 21 games out of first place, he believed they would turn things around and win the final 57 games.[39] He wasn't joking. Ronnie believed that the greatest turnaround in baseball history was possible.

The seasons of white in the church are the turnaround times for all of us. The message of Christmas and Easter is clear: it's not too late. The human race can turn things around. We can win the battle against sin and death. It seems impossible, because it *is* impossible. The Chicago Cubs have never won 57 games in a row. No one has done it, and no one ever will. Nor will human beings be able to conquer death or root out all traces of pride, envy, lust, anger, gluttony, sloth, and greed. And yet God has done for us what we could never do for ourselves. That is the miracle of Christmas and Easter. Paul exclaims in disbelieving wonder, "Thanks be to God, who gives us the victory through our Lord Jesus Christ" (I Corinthians 15:57). That same victory can be ours today. It is the greatest turnaround in human history.

---

[38] Pat Hughes and Rich Wolfe, *Ron Santo: A Perfect 10* (Taipei: Lone Wolf Press, 2011), 259.
[39] Ibid., 117.

CHAPTER 3. WHITE

"[I] was blind, but now I see," wrote former slave ship captain John Newton. He described God's goodness in words that millions know and love.[40] It is the experience that matters, however, more than the words. It is one thing to read the words of an advertisement: "For only $20 a month you can lose 20 pounds at Platinum Fitness." It is another thing altogether to perspire at the gym and feel the pounds melt away.

So what is the turnaround experience like? How does the Bible describe the astonishing change from purple to white, from sadness to joy? Here are a few of the metaphors from Scripture, images that help us imagine a new life in Christ.

1. SUNRISE. After stumbling in the dark, we are dazzled by the brilliant gold of the sun as it appears in the east.[41]
2. MARRIAGE. After dating and courting and seeking a life partner, we make our marriage vows. The two have become one.[42]
3. SURGERY. After trying familiar (and ineffective) home remedies, we submit at last to the surgery that we have long needed.[43]
4. SHELTER. After being alone and on the street, we find a place where everyone knows our name and says, "Welcome home."[44]

---

40 "Amazing Grace," lyrics by John Newton, music 19th century U.S. melody. Newton alludes to the dramatic story in John's gospel when a blind man is doubly healed. Not only does the blind man gain his eyesight, but he also gains insight into the meaning of the miracle. He discovers that Jesus is the true light coming into the world. See John 1:9, 9:25, 35–39.

41 Isaiah 60:1, I John 1:5–7, Revelation 21:22–24.

42 Mark 10:8, II Corinthians 11:2.

43 Matthew 9:10–12.

44 Psalm 23:6, John 14:2–3.

5. **FREEDOM.** After struggling with harmful habits and addictions that seem unbreakable, we are released from bondage. We are free at last.[45]
6. **BEAUTY.** After futile efforts to hide the stains and scars that are all too visible—to our embarrassment and shame—we are blessed with radiant beauty.[46]
7. Embrace. After injuring a loved one and finding ourselves **ESTRANGED**, we are now embraced with an open heart and open arms.[47]
8. **BIRTH.** After months of confinement in the womb, we are born into God's world.[48]
9. **ADOPTION.** After feeling like a motherless child, we are adopted into a family and treated as a son or daughter.[49]
10. **INNOCENCE.** After being charged with numerous offenses and admitting our guilt, we find ourselves acquitted. The judge declares us "Not guilty."[50]

There are other images in Hebrew and Christian Scripture that point to a dramatic turnaround: from lost to found (Luke 15:1-10), from war to peace (Romans 5:1-2), from ignorance to insight (Genesis 28:16). They are all pictures of new life, a new life that is healthy and victorious (like the championship of the Chicago Cubs

---

[45] Romans 6:16-18.
[46] Isaiah 1:18, Ephesians 5:25-27.
[47] Luke 15:11-25.
[48] John 3:3-7, I Peter 1:3.
[49] Romans 8:14-16, Galatians 4:4-6, Ephesians 1:4-5.
[50] Isaiah 55:7, Romans 3:21-26.

CHAPTER 3. WHITE

after 108 years of futility). New life means new adventures for us as children of God and disciples of Jesus.

But again, there is good news and bad news. The good news is that the joy of Christmas and Easter is a gift from God, a gift without strings or conditions. The offer of new life is made to everyone, including those who are hostile toward religion or bored or indifferent or self-serving. There is hope for all of us. The bad news is that the simple act of turning around is not simple at all. Just as the hour of sunrise is not within our conscious control, the hour of our spiritual awakening is not something we can consciously arrange. And here is the greatest difficulty of all: we are willing—yet unwilling—to surrender our self-will. Yes, we want to be blessed by God, but we still want to call the shots. We want God to do it our way.

We are like the man who tracked mud into his house and set about cleaning the mess, not realizing that because his boots were still muddy, his efforts made matters worse. As he wiped the kitchen floor, it became dirtier and dirtier. He had not removed his boots. The problem for us is that our will is permanently tainted. We may profess our love for God, but in the dark corners of our soul we continue to plead, "Not thy will, but mine be done." We can make a decision: "I want to clean up my life." But because our soul is muddy, we continue to rebel against God.

How can we possibly change? Only God can replace our inner darkness with radiant splendor. Only by God's grace can we be transformed.

B. WHITE SEASONS IN THE CHURCH

"White Christmas" has been a favorite Christmas song for decades. "I'm dreaming...," the song begins. We dream of a snow-covered world (before the snow turns to mush). We dream of a holiday "just like the ones we used to know" (before we were disillusioned by the grittiness of real life). We dream of a magical Christmas that will make us happy forever. But by the time we put away our holiday decorations, the magic is gone.

In a similar way many of us are stirred by the loveliness of springtime, "when weeds, in wheels, shoot long and lovely and lush,"[51] when Easter bonnets and Easter baskets announce that "It's time! It's time to celebrate rebirth in a world that has been homely and drab." Unfortunately, the bright anticipation soon fades, and the promise of Easter is soon forgotten.

How can our Easter longings and Christmas dreams come true? How can the two white seasons be more than a few weeks on the calendar, becoming instead the turning points that change everything? "I am making all things new," says the Holy One (Revelation 21:5). "But how?" we wonder.

CHRISTMAS

It all begins with a baby. When we cannot ascend to God, God descends to us. But why as an infant? Why not as a warrior, who can dazzle us into submission? Soren Kierkegaard's famous parable has been helpful for many of us. Suppose there was a king, Kierkegaard begins. The king is like no other ruler. He is able to crush all opponents. He is wealthier than anyone who has ever lived. And yet he is melted by love for a young woman, a woman with no prestige or power, a woman who lives in a forest cottage.

---

51   Gerard Manley Hopkins, *Poems and Prose* (Baltimore: Penguin, 1963), 28.

CHAPTER 3. WHITE

How can he declare his love for her? If he were to command her, "Come to the palace," she would yield to his wishes—no one dares to resist him! But would she love him? She would profess to love him, but would she truly? Would she live with him in fear, longing for her former life? Would she be happy at his side? How could he know? He wants a lover, an equal, not a cringing subject. And so he decides to approach her cottage incognito, wearing the cloak of a beggar. He leaves his throne and takes on a new identity, hoping to win her love without crushing her freedom.[52]

The Word became flesh, the Bible tells us (John 1:14), flesh that is fully human. "For we do not have a high priest who is unable to sympathize with our weaknesses, but we have one who in every respect has been tested as we are, yet without sin" (Hebrews 4:15). Christmas means that God has come to us incognito. God has been where we are and has felt what we feel. A well-known carol describes this willingness to descend: "He was little, weak, and helpless, tears and smiles like us he knew; and he feeleth for our sadness, and he shareth in our gladness."[53] God is willing to do whatever it takes to win our trust without coercing us.

Again, a parable helps us understand the gift of Emmanuel, God with us. The story is told by Lewis Cassels of an ordinary man who is too sophisticated for religion. He refuses to attend church with his family on Christmas Eve. "I'm a good and kind father," he tells himself. "I'm helpful in my community. Why should I worship a baby born in Bethlehem? I'm too honest to believe in

---

52　I am indebted to Philip Yancey, who retells Kierkegaard's parable in *Disappointment with God* (Grand Rapids: Zondervan, 1988), 103–104.

53　"Once in Royal David's City," lyrics by Cecil Frances Alexander, music by Henry J. Gauntlett, verse 3.

all that 'Jesus bit.'" So he sits by the fire on December 24, reading a novel, while his wife and children are at church. Late in the evening he hears thuds against his picture window. "Snowballs?" he wonders. He soon discovers that there are birds, drawn to the light from the window, hurling themselves against the glass. "They'll freeze," he realizes. "They need my help." Nearby is the heated garage. But it does no good to open the garage door and turn on the light. The birds keep flopping helplessly in the snow. He tries a trail of food to the garage door—to no avail. Then he tries to catch the birds, but his efforts are futile. "They don't understand me or trust me," he realizes. "If I could become a bird myself, if I could be one of them, then I could lead them, and they could be saved." Suddenly he hears the church bells at midnight, pealing the songs of Christmas morning. He sees in a flash of wonder the meaning of Christ's birth.

Becoming one of us—that is the breathtaking story that is told in late December and early January. For twelve days—December 25 through January 5—we dress our churches in white and marvel at the gift of "heaven to earth come down."[54] How do we respond? We may be like the residents of Bethlehem who thought: "Another baby born in poverty. That's nothing new." They missed the glory. Or we may be like the shepherds, who left their flocks and hurried to Bethlehem, allowing themselves to be amazed (Luke 2:16-18).

---

54 "Love Divine, All Loves Excelling," lyrics by Charles Wesley, music by John Zundel, verse 1.

CHAPTER 3. WHITE

EASTER

In a similar way the joy of Easter was perceived by some and missed by many. The empty tomb did not convince Peter that Jesus was alive. Not at first. Running to the tomb with John the son of Zebedee, he looked inside. Then he entered the place where Jesus' body had been laid. He saw the grave clothes folded neatly, but it made no sense to him. John had a flash of insight. Peter was not yet convinced.[55]

Nor did Mary Magdalene understand when Jesus himself appeared to her. This was her friend, her teacher, the one she admired and loved, and yet she did not recognize him. She assumed he was a landscaper. (Was she blinded by her tears? Was she so overcome with sadness that she glanced at Jesus but failed to pay attention?) Later, when he spoke to her by name, she knew: "He is alive!"

It was easy to miss the miracle. Many residents of Jerusalem on that first Easter morning did not see or believe. Many were absorbed in the ordinary chores of life and had no time for resurrection rumors. For us today the same dichotomy persists. Some can see beyond the Easter lilies and tulips to the glorious good news. Some cannot—at least not yet.

And so the church continues to proclaim the message, "He is not here; he has risen."[56] It is a bold and crucial message. In the words of Paul, "If Christ has not been raised, then our proclamation has been in vain and your faith has been in vain."[57] We know

---

55 John 20:3-10.
56 Luke 24:6 NIV.
57 I Corinthians 15:14.

that death is our enemy, our ultimate enemy.[58] If our enemy prevails in the end, what good is our striving? What good are our accomplishments? If everything is to be obliterated, swallowed in the void of non-being, we can carry on *as if* our life on earth matters, but we know, if we are honest, that life is a charade. In the words of Shakespeare: "It is a tale told by an idiot, signifying nothing."[59]

The question for Christians is simply "Do we serve a risen Savior? Is he in the world today?" If Jesus is merely a noble hero, to be revered at his tomb, like Abraham Lincoln or Martin Luther King, Jr., then we can feel gratitude for his life. We can be inspired to follow his example. But we cannot be confident or secure as we look to the future. "Because He Lives" has become a favorite hymn in many churches: "Because he lives, I can face tomorrow; because he lives, all fear is gone."[60] This is where the Christian faith ultimately stands or falls. It lives only as Christ lives.

Can we honestly believe that God's love is stronger than death? As we move into the white season of Easter, can we experience the joy that is beyond all earthly joys?

C. WHITE SEASONS IN ME

CHRISTMAS. Christmas came early for me. I was 13 years old, living in a new community. "Would you like to go to church camp?" I was asked. "Sure, why not?" I replied, not knowing that my life would be changed forever. Church camp, I discovered, was fun.

---

58 I Corinthians 15:26.
59 William Shakespeare, *Macbeth*, Act 5, Scene 5.
60 "Because He Lives," lyrics by Gloria and William J. Gaither, music by William J. Gaither.

CHAPTER 3. WHITE

There were hundreds of teenagers enjoying a college campus. The music was excellent. The classes were more challenging (and interesting!) than our Sunday School lessons back home. I was making new friends. There were even some attractive girls. But spiritually I was asleep. God was just a word for me, not a living presence in my life. And to tell the truth, I had no interest in what some might call a spiritual awakening. I was into school, sports, and classmates. I was not into being "holy."

Toward the end of the week I was interviewed by another teenager. It wasn't much of an interview. He said (or maybe it was a she—I don't remember), "I'm taking a class this week, and we're supposed to ask people, 'Are you a Christian?' What would you say?" For some unknown-to-me reason, I said no. I had attended church almost every Sunday of my life, but I was convinced that being a Christian should mean more than showing up and sitting in a church pew. It should be more exciting than that and more demanding. Whatever it was, it was beyond anything I could understand. "No, I'm not really a Christian," I told the young interviewer. The response was memorable: "What? You're at church camp. How can you not be a Christian?" I surmised that everyone else had answered yes. I was the odd one, the outlier. And that was fine with me. I had told the truth.

But the question was lodged in my soul. I began to wonder what it would be like to answer yes. What would it feel like? How would I know if I was a real Christian instead of a pew warmer? I thought about it off and on throughout the day. Then it was time for our closing worship service. "This service will be special," people were saying. What did that mean? I had no idea.

As the service began, we sang a stirring hymn: "Once to every man and nation / Comes the moment to decide / In the strife of truth with falsehood / For the good or evil side."[61] I had never heard the words, nor had I heard the melody. But as I sang with my fellow teenagers, I began to feel alive in a new way. I sensed that this was an invitation for me to give up my spiritual slothfulness. It was time to seek something—or Someone—bigger than myself. The sermon that night was equally electrifying for me. Every word spoken by Rev. Tom Whiting seemed wondrously fresh. His text was John 1:14: "And the Word became flesh and dwelt among us, full of grace and truth." I could not escape—nor did I want to escape—from a love so amazing, so divine. I said yes on that summer evening, yes to the birth of Christ within me. I found myself weeping for joy.

Unfortunately, it was such a profound experience that I was afraid to share it with others. I was a little bit embarrassed and quite a bit confused by what had happened. And so I filed it away in my memory bank, burying that luminous moment, returning to ordinary life as a teenager. But I *knew* at age 13 that God was real and alive and that someday I would figure out what to do with the glory I had seen. I had tasted the reality of Christmas in an unforgettable way.

EASTER. It had to be one of the sorriest Holy Week services in the history of Chicago. I came home on that Thursday evening, thinking to myself, "I'm not cut out to be a pastor. If I have to go through another experience like this, I'd be better off leaving the

---

61 "Once to Every Man and Nation," lyrics by James Russell Lowell, music by Thomas J. Williams. Lowell's poem was a vigorous protest against the U.S. war with Mexico in 1845.

CHAPTER 3. WHITE

church and leaving the ordained ministry." I was 27 years old, in my first year of leading (or trying to lead) a congregation. It wasn't a terrible year. My small congregation was patient and polite. But there was not much energy or passion or joy in the church—or I should say, there was not much energy or passion or joy in me.

I was surviving, treading water, until that fateful Thursday of Holy Week. I had never attended a Holy Week service—nothing that I could remember—and so I was excited about the possibilities. "I want tonight's service to be meaningful, maybe even powerful," I kept thinking. It was not meaningful. Nor was it powerful. It was a dud.

After an entire day of trying to write a sermon—an entire day!—I had completed one paragraph. I literally had nothing to say on that Maundy Thursday. That was bad enough. But the music that evening was disastrous. Our choir director, Dick Smith, decided that a men's quartet could sing "O Sacred Head, Now Wounded" *a capella*. There would be no accompaniment, just four male voices harmonizing. I don't know what caused the disaster, but someone began to sing off key. The other three singers kept going, even though one voice was butchering Bach's harmony. Finally, in the middle of the second verse, they stopped. They simply gave up and sat down.

I felt sorry for everyone who had come to church that night. They heard a pitiful one-paragraph sermon. They saw an embarrassing display of non-musical talent. I felt even sorrier for those who would be coming to our church on Sunday to celebrate Easter. What a letdown it would be. But since I was still employed by the church (I had not submitted my resignation), I sat down at my desk once again and managed to scribble out a message about Jesus "on the third day."⁶² My Easter sermon was nothing special. But Easter came to that congregation in spite of my human weakness. Why was that Easter spectacularly joyful? It's hard to say. It was not because I was a stellar preacher (I wasn't). Nor did we have a glorious choir (we didn't). Was the congregation on fire with spiritual passion? Not really. The only explanation that made sense to me was that Jesus was there. We somehow knew that Christ was alive in Chicago, Illinois.

I felt alive again as a pastor. The failures of Holy Week did not mean that our church was finished or that I needed to find new employment. In fact, our failures prepared the way for God to surprise us. Our dullness could not stifle the Spirit of the living God. I got the message: "Surprise! Easter can arrive in spite of our clunkiness."

D. THEOLOGY IN THE COLOR WHITE

TOO GOOD TO BELIEVE?
Theology in the color white is good news—the best good news. God does for us what we cannot do for ourselves. God also does in us—not only *for* us but also *in* us—what we long for in an ambivalent way. We want to be healed, but we are attached to the old patterns that made us sick. We are tired of the darkness in our life, but the darkness has less-than-honorable benefits that we enjoy. "No matter," says the Holy One. "I can bless you and transform your world." "How can that be?" we ask. God's answer in the white seasons is

---

62 "On the third day" is a key phrase in the New Testament, a phrase referring to the resurrection of Jesus. See Matthew 12:40, 20:18–19, Luke 9:22, 13:31–35, Acts 10:39–41, and I Corinthians 15:3–4.

justification[63] by grace through faith (Ephesians 2:8). Not simply "justification by faith," even though many Protestants have used those words as a battle cry. The problem with saying "by faith" instead of "by grace through faith" is that faith itself is a gracious gift from God, not a human achievement. To say "I am right with God because of my faith" is to imply that I have done something commendable to earn God's favor. It implies that I am special, because I have accepted the teachings of Scripture; therefore, God is rewarding me.

"No!" theologians have thundered, from Augustine to Luther to Reinhold Niebuhr. We do not—we cannot—buy from God the gifts that God freely offers. "Ah," some have said, "but we must choose to receive God's grace." "You don't understand," the theologians respond. "Our ability to choose is defective. You are falling into the Pelagian error that has always plagued the church. You are speaking as if it were a simple transaction: God offers, we accept. Good for God. Good for us. But it is never that simple."

Sin is so deeply rooted in our world (and in us) that we are not able to make a wholehearted, unequivocal decision to be transformed. It is the grace of God that brings us to a turning point moment, a moment of despair, a moment when we realize "I can never untangle the mess in my life." And when that moment comes, we collapse. We fall into the void of nothingness, only to discover

---

63 Justification is a New Testament word that fails to resonate with many 21st-century Christians. We think of politicians who try to justify their questionable behavior, and we think of teenagers who offer elaborate excuses or justifications for arriving home after midnight. Those are self-justifying behaviors, not at all like the good news that God has justified us, declaring us righteous. Paul explains the difference in Romans 8:31: "If God is for us, who can be against us?" If God has said that all is forgiven, that all is right between us and God, who can declare us guilty?

that we have been caught and held and delivered from sin and death. There is no merit in our desperate cry of "I give up." But when we finally let go of our need to be in control, there is a sigh of relief from heaven. "Now, at last," God says, "I can fill you with a new spirit of love and joy and peace." When we know that our cup is empty, God can bless us, so that our cup overflows. All is grace!

In the white seasons we are talking about justifying grace. Prevenient grace is the unfailing love of God that works behind the scenes in the purple seasons. Prevenient grace makes us hungry and restless. We are homesick, yearning for a home that we can't quite describe but that keeps tugging at our soul. Justifying grace, by contrast, turns on the light bulb. We see the goodness of God in Christ, perhaps gradually (some light bulbs have dimmer switches, so that the brightness can increase slowly) or perhaps in a brilliant flash. We discover that God has been waiting for us all along, calling us without trampling on our freedom or blasting us into submission.

Now it is clear! We realize that we are loved by the God of creation and that nothing we do or fail to do can call that love into question. We may be struggling spiritually; we may be foolish; we may be self-destructive; we may be cowardly; but God never loves us less.

"What must I do to be saved?" the Philippian jailer asks Paul (Acts 16:30). Paul replies, "Believe on the Lord Jesus ..." (Acts 16:31). He is not saying, "Prove that you are worthy by believing." He is not giving the jailer a test or asking, "Do you believe all the right doctrines?" He is simply telling a desperate man to believe the amazing good news revealed in Christ: we do not need to *do* anything to be saved. In fact, there is nothing we *can* do. In the words of Paul Tillich's classic sermon, the only thing God asks is this: "Accept the fact that you are accepted."[64] In other words, let yourself be perfectly loved. It's as if we have lived in a dark house with all the blinds drawn. The sun has been shining every day, but we haven't seen it. "Let me open the blinds," God is saying.

I hope that we can reclaim the word *justification*, even though it sounds bookish, like something on a high school vocabulary quiz or like something our prim Aunt Martha might say. When used in Scripture, justification is brimming with life and power. God tells us that we are justified, that we are no longer blemished or unhealthy or guilty or alienated or lost. Because of what Christ has done for us, we are considered (in the eyes of God, which is ultimately all that matters) thoroughly good and utterly pure. To "justify" in this sense is to make someone just or righteous.[65] This is astonishing news: "You are perfectly righteous as you live in Christ." "No way," we are tempted to respond. "I'm the same old mixture of faithful and foolish, self-giving and self-serving, generous and cold-hearted, dependable and spacy." But God answers, "You are now and have always been my beloved child. I see you as forgiven and healed. I see you as honored and worthy." "I'm sorry, Lord," we protest, "but you may be deluded. That's not me you are describing." "But it *is* you," God says. "Only believe."

It seems too good to be true, until we quit fighting. And when that day comes, when we surrender at last and allow the justifying grace of God to convince us, the party begins. We

---

64 Paul Tillich, *The Shaking of the Foundations* (New York: Scribner's, 1955), chapter 19.

65 "Justi-" is from the Latin word *justus*, meaning "just" or "righteous." The suffix "-fy" is from the Latin verb *facere*, meaning "to make."

are the prodigal ones, embraced and showered with gifts that dumbfound us. No longer are we living in the dreariness of purple. The world is dressed in brilliant white, a dazzling white that is a combination of all the colors. We are home. The holy God has welcomed us.

GOD'S UNCHANGING GIFT.

Gustav Aulen describes the crucifixion of Christ as a confrontation between good and evil, light and darkness.[66] The forces of evil won a decisive victory on Good Friday. God's champion was nailed to the cross, and the dark powers howled with glee. "It is finished," they heard Jesus say as he died,[67] and they were certain that in the battle of life against death, life was finished. Not only was Jesus' life over, but the ultimate destiny of the human race was settled. Death had prevailed.

The evil powers could not have guessed that Jesus' words on the cross were not a cry of defeat. He was saying that the ordeal was finished and that the reign of terror caused by death was finished and that the centuries of purple sadness were finished. In the cosmic battle between the Spirit of suffering love and the spirits of vindictive darkness, the Lamb of God had won a decisive triumph. The Book of Revelation tells us that the Lamb is at the heart of the throne.[68] That is to say, the ultimate power at the center of the universe is self-giving, self-sacrificing love. That love came down

---

[66] Gustav Aulen, *Christus Victor* (Eugene: Wipf and Stock, 2003). The original publishing date was 1956.

[67] John 19:30.

[68] Revelation 5:6-14.

CHAPTER 3. WHITE

at Christmas. That same love defeated the powers of death and darkness on Easter morning, as the disciples cowered in fear.

Justifying grace is God's Spirit opening our eyes and our hearts so that we are no longer blind and confused. We no longer wonder, "Is there a God?" or "Am I truly loved and forgiven?" We can now say yes to God's amazing grace.

DOUBT OR FAITH.
In the purple seasons we respond with denial ("It's not so bad; I don't need anyone's help") or repentance ("I give up; Lord, save me"). In the white seasons we respond with doubt ("What if it's not true? What if Christmas and Easter are fairy tales for children?") or faith ("Lord, I believe; help my unbelief").

Faith is always a matter of head and heart. If we follow our heart without honest and rigorous thinking, we become wishful thinkers, wishing without solid evidence. Mushy, mindless religion will not sustain us in the long run. On the other hand, if we rely only on logic, ignoring our heart, we soon discover that head religion is never adequate. Logic is like a pier extending into the ocean. When we come to the end of the pier, we are still surrounded by a vast expanse of water and sky. The human mind cannot possibly grasp all there is to know about this infinite expanse.[69] Head and heart together can bring us to a faith that is reasonable, without eliminating the need to trust and embrace the mystery.

---

69 I have long appreciated the words of G. K. Chesterton: "The poet only asks to get his head into the heavens. It is the logician who seeks the heavens into his head. And it is his head that splits." G. K. Chesterton, *Orthodoxy* (San Francisco, Ignatius, 1995), 22. The original publication date was 1908.

Believing means agreeing with our mind that the story of Christmas and the story of Easter make sense. The colors give us a framework for understanding our human dilemma (seasons of purple) and our hope for deliverance (seasons of white). But believing with our rational mind is not enough. Faith also means trusting. When we believe with our head and trust with our heart, God can change our world.

Saying yes to the good news is like falling into a clear, refreshing pool on a muggy, miserable day. With joy and delight we respond with "Ahhhhhhhh!" What could be better? "Behold," says the Lord of all creation, "I make all things new."[70]

---

70 Revelation 21:5 KJV.

CHAPTER 3. WHITE

QUESTIONS FOR DISCUSSION

1. Is joy different from happiness? If so, how would you explain the difference?

2. Do you believe that Christmas and Easter have made a difference in the world during the past 20 centuries? Have they made a difference in you?

3. Which of the biblical metaphors on pages 4 and 5 speak to you most meaningfully?

4. How would you explain "justification by grace through faith" to a person completely new to religion and Christianity? Is faith simply believing what the Bible says, or does faith involve something more than "correct beliefs"?

Chapter 4. GREEN

Green is the color of following Jesus in the world. In the green seasons we put our faith to work. Have we been greatly blessed? Yes! Therefore, we are not content to be spectators or couch potatoes.[71] We want to be people of action, doers of the word and not hearers only (James 1:22).

The color green is predominant in the church year, claiming more than 60 percent of our Sundays.[72] But Christians have little appreciation for the two green seasons, Epiphany and Pentecost, viewing them for the most part as seasons that merely fill the space after the more exciting times of Advent and Christmas, Lent and Easter. But the green seasons are not empty times, when nothing much happens. The 32 or 33 green Sundays are as significant as any during the year. Without green Sundays the beauty of Christmas and the joy of Easter would dissipate like fireworks that evoke wows but quickly vanish. The green seasons keep the spirit of Christmas and Easter alive.

---

71 Perhaps couch potatoes at church should be called pew potatoes.

72 The actual percentage of green Sundays varies, depending on whether there are 52 or 53 Sundays in the year and depending on the dates of Easter and Advent. Green Sundays range from a low of 60 percent to a high of 63 percent, more than 3 out of every 5 Sundays in the year.

And so I do not refer to the green Sundays as "Ordinary Time," even though the term is widely used. Ordinary Time sounds theologically bland. It's helpful, I think, to call the green seasons Epiphany and Pentecost, seasons that follow the Day of Epiphany on January 6 and the Day of Pentecost in May or early June.

For John Wesley the message of the green seasons was all-important. Wesley would say, if he were using the language of colors, that purple (repentance) and white (God's forgiveness) are of little worth without green (active discipleship). Think about a tomato seed planted in early spring. If the seed is buried in rich soil, that's good. If the seed germinates and a healthy shoot bursts into the sunlight, that's even better. But if the plant fails to grow, if it fails to yield a harvest of fresh tomatoes, the first two stages—planting and germinating—are for naught. The green seasons in the church challenge us to keep growing. After the seed of faith has been planted, the crucial question is always "What happens next?" Does the seed of faith flourish and eventually bear fruit? Does the purple of planting and the white of germinating lead to a harvest 30 or 60 or 100 times greater than what has been sown?[73]

We are talking here about spiritual growth in the real world. The mission of Jesus Christ extends far beyond our personal happiness to questions of "How can we provide sewers and sanitation in places where children die from preventable disease?" or "How can we protect the dignity of women, when they are victimized or abused?" or "How can we use biotechnology to benefit the human race while avoiding the pitfalls and perils?" Some would say that

---

73 See Matthew 13:23.

the church should stay clear of controversy and so-called secular entanglements. But the green seasons call us to move beyond our heart-warming experiences at the manger and our joyful astonishment at the empty tomb. The green seasons tell us to "put on the whole armor of God" (Ephesians 6:11), for there is work to be done. Often, of course, the work seems humdrum and ordinary, like nursing a baby or playing catch with an eight-year-old or shopping for a family cookout or listening to a frustrated colleague at work or repairing a faucet or attending a staff meeting. But if we are able to connect our faith with everyday life, then every day can be extraordinary. We can follow the way of Jesus with energetic vitality and see evidence of God's reign. On earth as in heaven.

A. THE GREEN SURPRISE

Imagine a house that has not been cared for since it was built in the 1950s. No routine maintenance. No repairs. No thorough cleaning of walls and windows. No pest control. The young family that lives in the house cannot afford an extreme makeover. There are two young children and a single mom, enduring cold drafts in the winter, a family of raccoons in the summer (the raccoons live above the ceiling and have fouled the 1950s insulation), rotting floor boards, and leaky plumbing. The neighbors have complained about the unpainted exterior. Finally, a city inspector arrives. The inspector has no choice but to condemn the entire structure. The young mother pleads with him. She is living on welfare and says, "I can't possibly pay rent elsewhere. This house is not in the best condition, but it belongs to me. I inherited it from my uncle, who wanted me to have a roof over my head. My husband vanished when I was pregnant for the second time, and there is no child support money. Please! Please let my family stay here! Don't condemn the only shelter that I can afford." The inspector is a kind man. "I'll see what I can do," he says. To the young mother's delight he returns in two weeks with what seems to be good news. "The city has decided not to condemn your home. You will not be evicted." The beleaguered mom is in tears. "How can I ever thank you?" she asks.

But the question remains: is the kind inspector doing a favor for this young family? Yes, he arranges for their deplorable living conditions to be passed over. Their notice of condemnation is forgiven by the authorities. But nothing has changed to improve their life. Their disaster of a home is as disastrous as ever.

John Wesley would say, "The family has not been fully saved. Their partial salvation is worth celebrating, but only if it is followed with a plan to make over everything in every room, from foundation to roof, from befouled insulation to clogged and leaky plumbing." In short, what good is forgiveness if it doesn't lead to a better life?

The green seasons in the church are a bold affirmation that God can save us "to the uttermost."[74] When the prodigal son returns as a shamed and shabby pauper, the father embraces him and gives him shoes ("you are not a servant; you are my son"), a robe ("you are honored and respected"), and a ring ("you have authority to make decisions in my name"). But the question has not been answered: what happens next? Is the younger son transformed by his father's incredible generosity? Does he become a responsible and loving son? Or does he continue to squander the family's

---

74 Hebrews 7:25 KJV.

property and abuse the family's trust? We don't know the answer, because Jesus' parable ends on Day One of the homecoming. What happens on Day Two?

"Wonderful news!" the Bible tells us. Not only are sinners forgiven. They also can experience an extreme makeover, a total transformation. Stubborn pride can eventually become courageous caring. Self-destructive habits can be replaced with a healthier lifestyle. Whatever was less than admirable—perhaps fornication, impurity, licentiousness, idolatry, sorcery, enmities, strife, jealousy, anger, quarrels, dissensions, factions, envy, drunkenness, and carousing[75]—can be changed. Not merely pardoned. Not merely overlooked by God. But radically changed. That is the good news we hear in the green seasons of our Christian life. It's the best possible news.

But how can this be? Are we kidding ourselves? Wasn't Martin Luther correct when he insisted that forgiven sinners are *simul justus et peccator*, at the same time righteous and sinful? We are righteous because Christ has died for our sins, but our sinful nature does not miraculously vanish. God loves us in spite of our spiritual messiness, but the mess remains. "Face the truth about yourself," Luther would say, pointing to the dark desires that are engrained in our human nature.

What would John Wesley say? He would agree that our sinful nature does not vanish overnight. The struggle continues for as long as we live. But we can hope for a radical transformation of our entire personality: heart, soul, mind, and strength. This is not

---

75 Galatians 5:19–21.

a vague hope, Wesley would say. We can anticipate God's making us perfect in love—in this life! This is a shocking affirmation. But Wesley was balancing his pessimism of nature (we cannot save ourselves) with an optimism of grace (God is able to save us, not partially, but completely). If God is repairing a dilapidated self, God will not walk off the job when the work is half done. It may take a lifetime. In fact, Wesley believed that almost no one reaches the state of perfect love until he or she is near the point of death. He never claimed it for himself. But unless we strive for perfection in love, we will be like a mediocre football team, content to win a few games each year, and never aspiring to excellence.

"Why not aim high?" Wesley is saying. Is God *able* to change us from self-centeredness to self-giving, from anxiety to radiant hope, from hollow pride to confident humility? Surely God is able. Is God *willing* to change us? Does God care enough to keep working with us until the victory is won? Surely God is willing. Is God *wise* enough to find a way to make it happen? Does God have an unlimited toolbox? Is the creative genius of the Holy One always at work, finding new ways to repair us? Surely God is creatively wise.

If we are overoptimistic, ignoring our human fallibility and foolishness, we will crash and burn, like Peter, who declared, "Though all become deserters because of you, I will never desert you" (Matthew 26:33). Peter learned the hard way. When it comes to human nature, Christians must remain pessimistic. But if we are overly pessimistic, putting limits on God's grace, refusing to believe that God is able enough, willing enough, and wise enough to change us, we will never soar as Christians. We will be like a Boeing 737 that taxis from the terminal to the end of the runway and then turns around, always taxiing, never flying, never doing what it was built to do. The secret of healthy growth for Christians is 100 percent pessimism ("I can't") combined with 100 percent optimism ("God can").[76]

B. GREEN SEASONS IN THE CHURCH

The least familiar season for most Christians is Epiphany, which begins on January 6 and continues until we enter the darkness of Lent. Epiphany is an expandable season, sometimes only four or five Sundays, sometimes as many as eight or nine Sundays, often six or seven Sundays. It all depends on the date of Easter. A very late Easter means a very long Epiphany; an early Easter means that Epiphany is squeezed and reduced. During Epiphany we remember the life and ministry of Jesus, from the arrival of the Magi with gold, frankincense, and myrrh, to his baptism and years of teaching and healing.

Pentecost, the other green season, seems to last forever. It begins in May or June, after the 50 days of Easter have been celebrated, and continues into late November or early December. Again, Easter can expand or contract these green Sundays. There can be as few as 23, when Easter is late, and as many as 27, when Easter is early. On the red-letter day of Pentecost, Christians receive "power from on high," enabling us to do what has always seemed impossible. We can turn the world—and ourselves—upside down.[77]

---

76 This combination is precisely the secret of Alcoholics Anonymous and all Twelve-Step groups. The First Step is a confession of our human powerlessness: "We admitted we were powerless...that our lives had become unmanageable." The Second Step is a remarkably positive affirmation: "[We] came to believe that a power greater than ourselves could restore us to sanity."

77 Luke 24:49, Acts 17:6.

Both green seasons are times of Spirit-anointed vitality. In the purple times we discover the painful truth about ourselves: "All have sinned ..." (Romans 3:23). In the seasons of white we discover the exhilarating truth about God: "For God so loved the world that he gave his only Son ..." (John 3:16). What happens next? We begin to live the truth that we have learned. We become disciples in training and disciples on the move, no longer paralyzed by our ever-present weakness, no longer content to be joyfully amazed. It's time for the rubber to meet the road. It's time for our words about faith to become consistent and courageous action.

EPIPHANY

Epiphany follows Christmas. After Jesus is born (we celebrate for 12 days), he grows "in wisdom and in years, and in divine and human favor."[78] Around the age of 30 he ventures from his home town of Nazareth to be baptized in the Jordan River. John the Baptizer has already announced that a Mighty One will appear, one whose sandals he is not worthy to carry.[79] Jesus's baptism is the launching of his ministry, when he is commissioned for the most daunting task ever attempted. His mission—if he chooses to accept it—is to heal a broken world.

The first step for Jesus is to recruit twelve ordinary people to be his team members. The team has to be trained, and so he begins at the beginning, telling them and then showing them how to bring sight to the blind (the literally blind and spiritually blind), how to

---

78 Luke 8:52
79 Matthew 3:11

CHAPTER 4. GREEN

bring release to the captives (those literally enslaved and those in bondage to destructive lifestyles), and how to bring good news to the poor (the economically deprived and the psychologically wounded). Jesus has only three years to prepare them, and they are slow learners. They continue to bumble and fail.[80]

Is it painful for Jesus to see how dull they are? He sounds deeply grieved in John, chapter 6, when many of his disciples turn back and no longer go about with him (vv. 66–67). When Peter boasts during their final meal together, promising that he will never fall away (Matthew 26:35), Jesus was surely grieving. Still, he remains confident that these twelve ordinary followers can tell his story to the nations and bring God's peace where there is hatred and fear. As he predicts Peter's betrayal, in the next breath he says, "Once you have turned back, strengthen your brothers" (Luke 22:32). He believes that the disciples can learn and eventually get it right.

And so the first green season of the Christian year is a time of learning—learning to follow Jesus. We are still bumbling disciples, but we are willing to grow by listening to the Holy One and stepping out in faith. "The one who believes in me will also do the works that I do and, in fact, will do greater works than these," he tells us (John 14:12). Is it possible? If so, we have a lot to learn! The green season of Epiphany is when we go back to discipleship school and prepare ourselves for new challenges.

---

80 It is remarkable that the New Testament does not glorify or glamorize the original disciples. Their mistakes and misunderstandings are described in vivid and painful detail. They argue with each other about who is the greatest, even as Jesus is approaching his death (Luke 22:24). Peter is rebuked as a spokesperson for Satan (Matthew 16:23). Jesus tells Philip in John 14:9: "Have I been with you all this time…and you still do not know me?" His closest friends fall asleep when he needs them most (Luke 22:45–46). "O ye of little faith" is an all-too-constant refrain in Jesus's teaching (Matthew 8:26, 14:31, 16:8, Luke 12:28).

PENTECOST

The learning continues. Always. But when the green Sundays after Pentecost arrive, it's time to move from the classroom to the real world. We have discovered our mission: the mission of the global church (to make disciples for Jesus Christ everywhere), the mission of our local congregation (to make disciples for Jesus Christ in our neighborhood), and our personal mission (to make disciples for Jesus Christ by discovering and using our talents and spiritual gifts).

My local church in Tucson sponsored a dialogue on immigration. (The *frontera*, the U.S. border with Mexico, is only an hour away.) But if we merely talk about immigration, we are like the disciples of Jesus prior to Pentecost. They were "classroom disciples." At some point we need to go beyond dialogues and conversations to do hands-on ministry. No one has ever learned to swim by watching a video. To learn to swim means entering the water. In the same way no one has ever learned to be a disciple without jumping into real-world action: listening to elderly neighbors or building a Habitat for Humanity home or providing legal aid or cooking meals or offering Twelve Step programs or teaching children to pray. The green of Pentecost combines evangelism (offering Christ) with compassion (caring for individuals in the Spirit of Christ) and justice (shaping economic and political and social and legal systems in ways that reflect the values of Christ).

None of this can be accomplished, or even attempted, by isolated individuals. Jesus called a *group* of followers together and taught them that *together* they were his body, his living presence in the world. When the story of the early church was recorded in the Book of Acts, the work of changing the world—from death and

CHAPTER 4. GREEN

despair to life and hope—had barely begun. The 28 chapters of Acts are encouraging. But what happens in the 29th chapter of Acts, the chapter we are still writing today? Are we having conversations about mission, or are we up to our elbows in *doing* mission?

I cannot simply copy the work of others as I serve Jesus Christ, because my gifts and passions may be quite different from their gifts and passions. But there is work that I *can* do, something that fits me uniquely and brings joy to the heart of God. I need the prayers and support of my church community. I need to be part of a team. That's what the green season of Pentecost is all about—vital ministry in the body of Christ. Together we can make our lives count for good.

C. GREEN SEASONS IN ME

EPIPHANY. When I finally gave up trying to be in charge of my life, I said yes to the way of Jesus. But I was a rookie. My knowledge of the Bible was limited to "baby food" from Sunday School and "head religion" from Davidson College and the University of Chicago. Serious Bible study was in order. I was like an emaciated prisoner of war, starving for meat and potatoes and homemade apple pie. I desperately needed to be nourished. And so I began with the 17 volumes of William Barclay's *Daily Study Bible*, a commentary for beginners. Ten pages a day was all I could absorb. But after 10,000 pages and three years of daily study, I was beginning to be familiar with the whole New Testament, not just the easy, often-quoted verses. Then I decided to tackle the Old Testament in a disciplined way. I filled notebook after notebook with my questions and observations. Instead of limiting myself to what the experts saw in Deuteronomy or Isaiah, I read every chapter and verse for myself, trying to hear the voice of God through the words of human authors. I continued for years, journeying through the entire Bible again and again. It was seldom boring, because Bible study is like exploring the Grand Canyon—there is always something new to discover.

But digging in to the treasures of Scripture is not sufficient for disciples in training. Another surprise was in store for me when I was invited to join a small group of fellow clergy and religious professionals.[81] Our purpose was to explore the issues we faced in our daily work so that we could connect our external problems (a budget crisis or an angry staff member) with our internal needs and longings. This meant going deeper—much deeper—than most of us had ever gone, into the murky depths of our psyches. The group leader was wise and competent. We were able to name our demons and delight in our emerging gifts. It was a green season of Epiphany for me, as I committed myself to learning. I was exploring not only the written word of the Bible, but also the mystery of God's living word in the depths of my soul. There were some monsters to be confronted, but there was unfamiliar beauty as well.

PENTECOST. It's easy to coast in our spiritual life after we've been at it for a while. The green Sundays after Pentecost have reminded me that there's more to be attempted and more to be accomplished. "But Lord, I'd like to rest," I said after retiring from the relentless responsibilities of pastoring a church. "We'll see," the Lord seemed to be saying.

---

[81] We met at a local convent for two hours every month, except for one month in the spring and one month in the fall, when we spent a full 24 hours together.

CHAPTER 4. GREEN

I had moved to my new home in Tucson in October 2011. Within days of the move, I was invited to meet with Reverend Mike Pearson, the district superintendent in Southern Arizona. (How did he know I was in town? I had no idea. I had not announced my presence.) Mike took me to a nearby restaurant, asked questions about my recent retirement, and then hit me broadside with an unexpected challenge: "Are you ready to offer Spanishtown here in the Desert Southwest?" Somehow he had heard about my Spanishtown work in Illinois and Florida.

Spanishtown had been an exciting experiment for me. I had created the program so that church leaders could be completely immersed in Spanish, 14 hours a day, from Sunday evening to Friday noon. The effectiveness of the program had been remarkable, not only for the "pilgrims" (English speakers learning a new language) but also for the "guides" (native speakers present with us full time, a guide for every pilgrim).

But the truth was that I was *not* ready to continue with Spanishtown. It had been a drain on my psyche and on my bank account. I was worn out with all the logistical details: recruiting, transporting, overseeing an emotionally intense five days, trying to make ends meet financially.

"It's over," I wanted to tell Mike Pearson. But deep within, I sensed that God wanted me to continue an essential ministry. "Oh well, maybe," I heard myself saying. A few weeks later I had a committee. We chose a location for Spanishtown at a monastery in St. David, Arizona. Money was allocated by the Hispanic Ministry Committee in Phoenix—no more financial hardship. And eight months later it happened, one of our best Spanishtowns ever. It was a joy, in spite of my early reluctance. When God calls, God empowers. And when God empowers, there can be a harvest of good fruit and gladness.

D. THEOLOGY IN THE COLOR GREEN

WHO'S AFRAID OF BEING HOLY?

Many of us would feel embarrassed or insulted to be called "holy." Holy people are often perceived as abnormal, officious perhaps, otherworldly for sure. Nuns are holy, so it is believed; women who live ordinary lives (working downtown, driving in carpools, taking yoga classes) are not. Missionaries are holy, so it is believed; regular church members who work in corporations or high schools or fire stations are not. Anyone who claims to be holy is likely to be branded as arrogant or dangerous.

The problem may be semantic. When we hear the word "holy," we think of a distasteful phrase: holier than thou. But Christlike holiness has absolutely nothing to do with the self-preening righteousness that Jesus condemned. Many of Jesus' enemies were indeed holier than thou, taking pride in their religious trappings but never realizing what was spiritually (and sadly) absent.[82] They were substituting an external costume for authentic spirituality.

John Wesley urges us to reclaim the biblical vision of holy living affirmed in Hebrews 6:14: "Pursue peace with everyone, and the holiness without which no one will see the Lord." Purity of heart is where holiness begins.[83] As we learn to love God with our

---

82 See, for example, Luke 11:39–41, Matthew 6:1, 5, 16, and Matthew 23:23–31.

83 The beatitudes of Jesus make this clear, especially Matthew 5:8: "Blessed are the pure in heart, for they will see God."

CHAPTER 4. GREEN

entire being, and as we learn to care deeply about God's world, we become more and more Christlike in our behavior. We discover new ways to *do* our faith instead of talking about our faith in a pompous or preachy way. If holiness is authentic, it is never preachy. It is infused with humility, not seeking the limelight, not puffing itself up with self-importance.

We are talking here about real-life sainthood. Again, the word "saint," like the word "holy," has been corrupted. Real saints, we imagine, are dead people who were somehow perfect. They never succumbed to temptation, so we think, or made fools of themselves or uttered an angry word or failed to be spectacular. "Wrong!" the New Testament keeps reminding us. Every disciple—Saint Peter, Saint Paul, Saint John, Saint Matthew, and all the rest—had bad days. After years of leadership in the church, Saint Peter had to be chastised by a fellow apostle when he practiced unholy discrimination against Gentile Christians.[84] But this former fisherman, still far from perfect, was a man of holiness. He loved God and he loved people. He was eager to grow as a follower of Christ.

Some have used the word "wholly" to describe what it means to be holy. Are we willing to give ourselves wholly to God's way of compassion and justice? Are we willing to say, "Yes, Lord, I want to be wholly yours"? Or do we give a smidgen of ourselves, loving the Lord our God with a fraction of our heart, a small portion of our soul, an isolated section of our mind, and an occasional donation of our strength? Do we sort of love our neighbors, provided it is convenient and pleasant for us?

---

84 Galatians 2:11–14. This is a fascinating and enlightening story that is little known and seldom discussed in sermons or Bible study classes.

The biblical standard of holiness is not optional, Wesley reminds us. God cares enough for our well-being to declare unequivocally, "You shall be holy, for I am holy" (I Peter 1:16). God wants us to thrive, and when we aim for God's will to be done *wholly* on earth (and *wholly* in us), we become our best selves. We do not become holier-than-thou Pharisees. We become holy people whose messy souls and impure hearts are being transformed by the living God. We are holy *now*, if we have welcomed the Holy One into our life.[85] But we have a long way to go to become filled to the brim with God's goodness and strength and wisdom. Are we holy now? Yes, by God's grace. Are we still growing in holiness? Always. How can both be true at the same time? How can we be saints if we are not yet saintly in our attitudes and habits?

WHITE AND GREEN TOGETHER: A DOUBLE GIFT FROM GOD. The white of Christmas and the white of Easter tell us that we have been embraced by God. The Holy Child of Bethlehem has descended to us, simply because God loves us. No reasons are given. No reasons are needed. And when we fail as disciples, when we abandon the Holy One as he is scorned and crucified, God does not reject us. "Go, tell his disciples and Peter that he is going ahead of you to Galilee" (Mark 16:7). Even Peter, who denied Jesus after boasting that he would never fail, is welcomed home by the Lord of Easter, no questions asked. The color white offers an astounding gift: the justifying grace of God, forgiving us when we don't deserve

---

85 One of the most stirring promises in all of Scripture is made by Jesus in John 14:23: "Those who love me will keep my word, and my Father will love them, and we will come to them and make our home with them."

CHAPTER 4. GREEN

to be forgiven, pardoning us when we are at our worst, treating us as if we were faithful, when in fact we have flopped. The word "justification" has been defined as the love that welcomes us, *just as if* we had never sinned. Our beauty may not be visible. It may be hidden, smudged, covered over, and difficult to discern. But God sees what we can become and says to us at Christmas and Easter, as God said to Jesus when he was baptized, "You are my child, the beloved; with you I am well pleased."[86] When the Holy Child of Bethlehem lives in us, we share in his holiness. When the Lord of Easter enters our life, his radiance becomes visible in us. This is what theologians call imputed righteousness. God sees us as wealthy when it comes to goodness, even though we are paupers. It is as if the goodness of Jesus has been deposited in our "goodness account." That makes us wealthy indeed!

But the green seasons bring an additional gift, a gift that is equally astonishing. They tell us that we can become truly good (not semi-good), wholly pure (not halfway pure). The second gift from God is known as imparted righteousness. Imputed righteousness is a fiction: the guilty ones are blessed, *as if* they were innocent; the undependable ones are embraced, *as if* they were dependable. Imparted righteousness is authentic innocence and real-life dependability. The ramshackle house that is our soul is being remodeled—completely. The spiritual mud that we have been spreading for years (through pride, envy, gluttony, greed, lust, sloth, and anger) is being scrubbed away, a laborious task that no longer seems hopeless.

---

86 When we are baptized into Christ, the words spoken to the Son of God in Mark 1:11 can be addressed to us. We become God's adopted sons and daughters.

The cleanup is accomplished by what we call the sanctifying grace of God. Prevenient grace says, "Wake up! You have wandered away from home." Justifying grace says, "Let's celebrate! You are home at last." Sanctifying grace says, "There's work to be done! Let's make the entire world a welcoming and loving home." The ultimate goal is boldly declared in Revelation 11:15: "The kingdoms of this world are become the kingdoms of our Lord, and of his Christ; and he shall reign for ever and ever."

It cannot happen unless we ourselves become Christlike.[87] The regeneration of the world begins with the regeneration of my own mind and spirit. That remolding and remaking begins in a conscious way during the white seasons, when I am justified by God and welcomed home. It continues in the green seasons, as I claim the remarkable words of assurance in Philippians 1:6: "The one who began a good work among you will bring it to completion by the day of Christ Jesus." This promise is not based on childish hopes or fanciful dreams. It is guaranteed to us in God's word.

What will it be like, the transition from darkness (purple) to dawn (white) to the full light of day (green)? It will be like divine surgery for each of us and for our planet. The illness is life-threatening (purple), and so God requires major surgery, which is the turning point (white), followed by gradual rehabilitation and recovery (green). It will be like emerging from the confinement of the womb

---

87 II Peter 1:4 declares that we can be "partakers of the divine nature," living not only *for* Christ but also *in* Christ. The Eastern Orthodox tradition has held fast to this core teaching through the centuries. Sometimes called "divinization," the concept is less confusing, I believe, if we remember that our human nature remains human. We do not become "little gods" when we are filled with God's Spirit. Rather, we are gradually transformed, so that we can reflect the light and love and courage of Christ.

CHAPTER 4. GREEN

(purple), experiencing the miracle of birth (white), followed by years of growing and maturing (green). It will be like the American Civil War (purple), coming to an end at Appomattox (white), requiring the arduous work of rebuilding a nation (green). All three colors are essential. All three stages are part of God's plan for us and for our world. The question becomes: how do we respond?

AVOIDING THE TWO DITCHES.
God gives us the ability to change. We can change as individuals, and we can work together for change in the world. We are not coerced by God, nor do we coerce others to accept the gift of new life in Christ. But when we discover the amazing grace that underlies the entire universe—prevenient, justifying, and sanctifying—we are like a young adult falling in love for the first time. We are overjoyed and grateful!

There are two pitfalls for us, however, as we respond to God's sanctifying grace, the transforming power that inspires us and motivates us and purifies us from within. I call them the two ditches. Imagine driving across Everglades National Park and Big Cypress National Preserve. The road is smooth and straight. It crosses one of the most desolate areas in the United States, about 60 miles of barrenness. When the granddaughter of a friend lost control of her car on this South Florida highway, she found herself sinking in the swampy water. The lesson was clear: if you drive on this road, you need to pay attention! If you drift off to the right, you can lose your car in a swampy ditch. If you drift off to the left, the result can be the same—sad news for you and your car.

The life of faith is similar to the road across the Everglades and Big Cypress or any road we happen to travel. On both sides of the roadway there are ways to have an unfortunate experience. In Hebrew Scripture the warning is given: "Do not swerve to the right or to the left; turn your foot away from evil."[88] The ditch on the right is not identical to the ditch on the left, but both are equally damaging to our health and well-being.

In the green seasons of our spiritual life the two ditches are polar opposites. On one side is the ditch of carelessness. In John Wesley's day this ditch was called antinomianism. The Bible refers to this danger in Romans 6:1-2 when Paul asks the 1st-century church (and the church in every century): "Should we continue to sin in order that grace may abound? By no means!"

When we are careless, we are cavalier in response to God's unfailing love. "God loves me unconditionally," we affirm correctly. "There is nothing I can do to make God stop loving me." True. But we are tempted to add: "Therefore it doesn't matter what I do. I can take it easy. I won't fret about what God requires. I'll do as I please, secure in the knowledge that I am eternally blessed." This is a dangerous ditch. Once we have been brought into the family of God with open arms—no matter who we are, no matter what we have done—we are called to be responsible members of the family, serving as we have been served. If we are truly grateful for the blessings we have received, we will want to be a blessing for others, not a slacker.

The second ditch that can ensnare us is compulsiveness. When we are serious about our faith, desiring to please God in all we do, the result may be a compulsion to overachieve. We may take on

---

88 Proverbs 4:27. See also Deuteronomy 5:32, 28:17, Joshua 1:7.

responsibility that does not belong to us. "I want to be my best self in response to God's grace," many of us say (appropriately). "I don't want to be a half-hearted Christian, a lukewarm believer, because God has said that if we are neither hot nor cold, we will be cast aside, spit out of God's mouth.[89] And so I will aim high. I will aim to be like Christ. I will aim to see the entire earth transformed." Those are worthy desires, far more worthy than the laissez-faire, anything-goes approach of careless Christians. But compulsive Christians miss the point in an equally damaging way. By being overresponsible for their life as disciples, they take on burdens that no human being can bear. They try to do God's part in changing the world instead of simply doing their part and trusting God to do the rest. Their hard work is admirable, but their work is anxious labor. Instead of living with serenity, they are troubled with persistent worries: "Have I done enough? Am I effective enough in my efforts? I'm working so hard, Lord. Why isn't the world responding? What else should I do?" The spirit of gratitude and joy is swallowed up by inner turmoil.

Neither ditch is acceptable for us as disciples of Jesus. Overresponsibility is as harmful as underresponsibility. The ditch of carelessness cheapens the grace of God, making grace nothing more than "whatever you do is fine with God." The ditch of compulsiveness denies that grace even exists, declaring, "If it is to be, it's up to me." Cheap grace and no grace. How can we avoid both errors?

The answer is graceful discipline and disciplined grace. God's love is not mushy or flabby. It frees us to be our best self and works

---

89 Revelation 3:16.

with us as we learn to be effective and useful. God never gives up on us, poking us and prodding us (purple seasons) and startling us with unimaginable love (white seasons) and challenging us to be about our Father's business in the real world (green seasons).[90] We are talking here about tough love, which is the only kind of love that can help us. The tough basketball coach who truly cares about every player will be far more effective than the good buddy coach who requires nothing at all.

So how do we respond as Christians in a world where both ditches are always threatening? To avoid the ditch of compulsiveness, we need a leap of faith. We need to let go each day and relax into the arms of God. "I am the Almighty God," our Lord reminds us, "able to fulfill your highest hopes and accomplish for you the brightest ideal that ever my words set before you. There is no need for paring down the promise until it squares with human probabilities.... All possibility lies in this: I am Almighty God."[91]

To avoid the ditch of apathy, we need to use the small-step approach, which sets attainable goals—small goals at first and then additional goals that enable us to be always "pressing on the upward way."[92]

When we have no goals, we become lazy Christians. When we have challenging goals, we can grow as Christians, provided that our efforts are undergirded by grace. Discipline without grace leads

---

90 Jesus described his "green season" purpose in the alternate reading of Luke 2:49: "Did you not know that I must be about my Father's business?"

91 Marcus Dods, quoted in Ray Ortlund, *Three Priorities for a Strong Local Church* (Waco: Word, 1983), 14.

92 This phrase is taken from the first verse of "Higher Ground," lyrics by Johnson Oatman, Jr., music by Charles Hutchinson Gabriel.

to misery. Grace without discipline leads to self-indulgence. But when discipline is grace-filled, we can delight in the green seasons of discipleship. The green seasons are wonderfully described by songwriter Michael Card:

> *There is a joy in the journey, there's a light we can love on the way.*
>
> *There is a wonder and wildness to life, and freedom for those who obey."*[93]

Wonder and wildness. What a journey it is! And what a journey it continues to be, until at last we are at home in the house of the Lord. Forever.

---

[93] Michael Card, "Joy in the Journey," 1994.

QUESTIONS FOR DISCUSSION

1. Why is "perfection in love" seldom talked about in the church today? Is it possible for this core teaching of John Wesley to inspire us in the 21st century, as it inspired Methodists in the past? Do you know anyone who truly aspires to sainthood? Is the desire to become a saint healthy or unhealthy?

2. Is the ditch of apathy (laziness) or the ditch of compulsiveness (overresponsibility) more troublesome for you? What can you do—with the support of others—to avoid both dangers?

3. Can you remember a time when you were growing spiritually, learning (as in Epiphany) or serving (as in Pentecost)? What helped you grow? What hindered you in your growth as a follower of Christ?

4. Imputed grace is different from imparted grace. How would you explain the difference?

Chapter 5. RED

The color red is altogether different from the sadness of purple, the joy of white, and the grateful discipline of green. Purple, white, and green describe our human experience:

1. We admit our spiritual poverty (purple).
2. We are blessed with the riches of God's love (white).
3. We learn to follow Christ as active, growing disciples (green).

These three basic colors provide a spiritual roadmap for us. Can we expect purple seasons of discouragement and confusion? Yes, for as long as we live. Does God surprise us with white seasons of gladness? Yes, often when we least expect it. What about the green seasons of our life, when we are learning to grow and serve as followers of Jesus? Yes, all three colors will help us find our way.[94]

---

94 Without a spiritual roadmap, we can drift into the hollowness that T. S. Eliot describes so eloquently: "We are the hollow men / We are the stuffed men / Leaning together / Headpiece filled with straw. Alas! / Our dried voices, when / We whisper together / Are quiet and meaningless / As wind in dry grass / Or rats' feet over broken glass / In our dry cellar." Eliot, "The Hollow Men" (1925).

But red is different, because it does not symbolize a spiritual season. It does not represent the purple of Advent (waiting in the dark) or the white of Christmas (seeing the light of Christ) or the green of Epiphany (learning to follow the light). It does not represent the purple of Lent (stumbling in the dark—again!) or the white of Easter (being raised from death into a brilliant new day) or the green season after Pentecost (learning to share God's light, so that we can bring hope and healing to others). Red, by contrast, points to the power that makes our spiritual journey possible. It is the color of the Holy Spirit, the gift that underlies every spiritual experience and leads us from purple ("I once was lost") to white ("but now am found") and then to green ("and grace will lead me home").[95]

Red symbolizes the living presence of God. "Taste and see," the Bible tells us, "that the Lord is good."[96] But our awareness of God is like our awareness of the ocean, as we stand on the shore. Yes, we have an idea of what the ocean is like, as we watch the waves roll in. The ocean, however, like the majesty of God, is always greater than our experience.

In a burst of stunned amazement, Paul praises the One who is not like us, the One who is Holy Mystery: "O the depth of the riches and wisdom and knowledge of God! How unsearchable are his judgments and how inscrutable his ways!" (Romans 11:33). Job experiences a similar awe as he hears God's voice from the

---

95 The words in parentheses—from "Amazing Grace," verses 1 and 3—are familiar to most church attenders and to many non-attenders. Why is "Amazing Grace" such a popular hymn, even in non-religious settings? Perhaps a longing for grace is built into our human nature. Perhaps we sense that we are lost and blind and that only a Higher Power can lead us into the welcoming light of home.

96 Psalm 34:8.

CHAPTER 5. RED

whirlwind, overwhelming him and causing him to repent in dust and ashes.[97] We are talking here about a power beyond anything we can grasp with human words. This is what the color red symbolizes: the God of Israel, the God of Jesus Christ, the God who brought into being a universe of billions of galaxies (as many as 140 billion), each containing billions of stars.[98] This God of unimaginable greatness is here. Now. Able to fill us with all that we need for happiness and well-being.

The original followers of Jesus were told to wait in Jerusalem until they received "power from on high" (Luke 24:49). "I will not leave you orphaned," he had told them earlier, promising to send another Advocate, a Helper to be with them forever.[99] The very Spirit of God would be poured out upon them so that they could be "partakers of the divine nature,"[100] having the mind of Christ,[101] doing what Christ himself had done,[102] and making disciples everywhere.[103] Without the power of the Holy Spirit, promised to those first disciples and to us, there would be no church, no community of believers, either then or now. The breath of God's Spirit is as essential for our life of faith as oxygen is essential for our physical life.

And so the color red is an emphatic reminder that the Holy Spirit is everywhere available. There is no shortage of God's power

---

97 It is a wonder that God speaks to Job. But when God's voice is heard at last (see Job 38-42), Job cowers in holy reverence and dread.

98 Bill Bryson, *A Short History of Nearly Everything* (New York: Broadway, 2003), 27.

99 John 14:17-18.

100 II Peter 1:4.

101 I Corinthians 2:16.

102 John 14:12

103 Matthew 28:19.

and love. But unlike our physical bodies, which breathe automatically (thanks to our autonomic nervous system), our spiritual life requires intentional openness to the Holy One. God's Spirit can fill us with new life moment by moment, but our minds and hearts must be open.

A. THE COLOR THAT CHANGES THE WORLD

When God sets out to change the world—from conflict to peace, from sorrow to gladness—God begins with individuals. People like us. We are brought together in faith communities and are given a clear mission: "Go therefore and make disciples of all nations, baptizing them in the name of the Father and of the Son and of the Holy Spirit, and teaching them to obey everything that I have commanded you" (Matthew 28:19–20). In these words that we know as the Great Commission of Jesus, there is only one main verb in the original Greek. The main verb is not "go" or "baptize" or "teach." (All three are participles in the Greek New Testament.) Instead, the main verb is a single word that we translate in English with a two-word phrase: "make disciples."[104] How do we accomplish that primary task? How do we make disciples? First, by going: going out to where people are wandering through life without a sense of ultimate purpose or direction. Second, by baptizing: baptizing isolated individuals into a community of authentic love and life-changing shalom. Third, by teaching: teaching slow-to-learn human disciples how to live as one family, serving each other, trusting each other, encouraging each other, laying down their lives for each other.

---

104 I am grateful to Robert E. Coleman for helping me understand the verbs used by Jesus in Matthew's Great Commission.

CHAPTER 5. RED

"Can it ever happen?" we wonder, as we watch our political leaders snipe and bicker. Meanwhile, global tensions threaten to erupt in devastating violence. Can the world be permanently transformed? The answer, in the words of Jesus, is "No" and "Yes." If we rely on our human strength and human wisdom, "No." ("Apart from me you can do nothing," he tells us in John 15:5.) But the answer is "Yes" if we are willing to be transformed from within. ("For God all things are possible," says Jesus in Matthew 19:26. Not some things, but all things!)

The color red tells us that God's Spirit can be poured out on "all flesh."[105] And so we pray for the living Spirit of God to fall afresh on us—and on all believers everywhere—so that we can become fully engaged disciples. This prayer has been set to music: "Melt me, mold me, fill me, use me."[106] "Melt me" expresses our yearning for change. Our stubborn habits are like cold iron that cannot be reshaped until they are placed in the fire of God's all-consuming love. "Mold me" is a plea for God to make us more like Christ. He is the pattern for human life at its best. "Fill me" is a confession that we are empty, that we are desperate for a clean heart, that we need a new and right spirit. Our request is simple and direct: "I need *your* life, *your* Spirit, *your* goodness, O Lord." Finally, we pray: "Use me." We step forward like Isaiah, who saw the Lord high and lifted up and responded with words of bold commitment: "Here am I; send me."[107]

---

[105] The two words, "all flesh," in Joel 2:28 and Acts 2:17 are often overlooked. God's Spirit is not a scarce resource, available for extraordinary believers and spiritual superachievers. "All flesh" means that *all* are invited to share in God's reign: the likely ones and the unlikely ones, including the ones we would never choose as brothers and sisters in God's family.

[106] "Spirit of the Living God," lyrics and music by Daniel Iverson.

[107] Isaiah 6:8.

Why are so many in traditional churches afraid of the Holy Spirit? Prior to the first decade of the 20th century, when the Pentecostal movement began to sweep across North America and eventually across the entire world,[108] the Holy Spirit was often forgotten or ignored. The term "Holy Ghost," an unfortunate choice of words in the Western world, was sometimes used. ("Holy Ghost" made God's Spirit sound spooky and alien to everyday life.) Then came the Pentecostals and Charismatics, who made the Holy Spirit relevant once again. Many of them insisted, however, on *glossolalia*—speaking in tongues—as a requirement for all Christians, and many of them delighted in unusual phenomena, like being "slain in the Spirit."[109] Non-Pentecostals, who might have been open to a fresh experience of the Holy Spirit, were scared away.

And so churches today often suffer from blandness and lethargy. The old story is still told about a small town church that had a defective furnace. The building caught fire, and the entire community came out to watch the efforts of the fire department. The preacher was there as well, praying that the fire could be contained. Suddenly the preacher noticed Walt, the owner of the local gas station, standing nearby. "It's good to see you, Walt," he said. "You're back at church for the first time in years." Walt replied, "Well, Preacher, this is the first time I've seen a fired up church."

It's the Spirit of the living God that turns bland churches into fired up congregations. The Spirit makes God's *power* visible in

---

108 For a brief yet thorough account of the Pentecostal movement in the 20th century, which has reshaped the church in Asia, Africa, and Latin America, see Richard J. Foster, *Streams of Living Water* (New York: Harper One, 1998), 112-127.

109 The person who is "slain" falls to the floor and appears to lose consciousness.

CHAPTER 5. RED

us[110]—power to persevere in doing all the good we can, by all the means we can, in all the ways we can, at all the places we can, to all the people we can, as long as ever we can.[111] An inexhaustible supply of power is promised in Luke 24:49. God's *wisdom* will also be clearly visible[112]—wisdom to listen more and talk less, wisdom to seek the well-being of the secular communities where we live,[113] wisdom to use our unique gifts to build healthier institutions and healthier relationships. But power and wisdom are of little value unless God's *love* is present. Without genuine love, our preaching is irrelevant, our serving is tainted, and our caring for each other is superficial. God promises for us a never-ending supply of *agapē* love, the self-giving love of Christ.[114]

The color red declares to us that we are upheld and empowered by the One who is able to do far more than all we can ask or imagine (Ephesians 3:20). *Veni, Sancti Spiritus*. Come, Holy Spirit. There is no other way for our efforts in the church to succeed.

B. THE CHURCH'S RED-LETTER DAY

Pentecost Sunday is the red-letter day that put Christmas and Easter on the calendar. If there had been no rushing wind and no tongues of fire in 1st-century Jerusalem,[115] the birth of Jesus

---

[110] Luke 24:49.

[111] Using words similar to these, John Wesley exhorted early Methodists to make their lives count for good.

[112] John 16:13.

[113] In Jeremiah 29:7 the people of Israel are told to seek the welfare of the city where they have been sent into exile. They are told to pray to the Lord on its behalf.

[114] John 15:9.

[115] The dramatic story is told in the first 41 verses of Acts, chapter 2.

would have been long forgotten. The resurrection of Jesus would be unknown except as a minor footnote in textbooks of ancient history. ("Certain Jews claimed that their teacher returned to life after being crucified," the textbooks might say.) But because the beleaguered disciples were inspired (or "in-spirited") on the Day of Pentecost twenty centuries ago, the name of Jesus is known and honored throughout the world. Those who worship Jesus as Lord and Christ owe their faith to this red-letter day, when God's Spirit became known in a surprising new way.

Pentecost was a major festival for 1st-century Jews. When Pentecost pilgrims by the thousands arrived in Jerusalem less than two months after Jesus' death, few of the pilgrims were aware that a rabbi from Nazareth had been admired and resented: admired by people who were "nobodies," resented by religious authorities who eliminated him. Now, fifty days later, the Feast of Pentecost was proceeding as usual. Suddenly it was far from a usual day. More than a hundred followers of Jesus were in the streets of Jerusalem, on fire with a message of urgent good news. In turn, more than 3,000 people were deeply moved by the message, deciding to be baptized on that red-letter day. The Christian movement was officially launched, a movement that now claims two billion adherents. No one can say how many of the two billion are devoted disciples, but there are certainly hundreds of millions.

It all goes back to that first Day of Pentecost. Why, then, is the Day of Pentecost such a non-event in most churches? Why are the white season holidays—Christmas and Easter—so exciting for Christians, while the red season holiday is barely noticed. Yes, there are efforts in some congregations to be creative on Pentecost Sunday, and many of the efforts have been noteworthy.

CHAPTER 5. RED

Some churches have used the recorded sound of a mighty wind. Others have included multiple languages in worship, recalling the miracle of communication in 1st-century Jerusalem.[116] There are choirs that process on Pentecost Sunday, following a kite in the shape of a dove. (The dove is suspended from an expandable pole and soars dramatically above the congregation.) Balloons and festive banners are often used, and congregation members are sometimes encouraged to dress in bright red to celebrate this red-letter day. But almost no one would say that Pentecost rivals Christmas and Easter in bringing excitement (and larger attendance!) to our churches. Pentecost Sunday is by and large just another day on the calendar, having little impact on anyone or anything in the typical congregation. How sad! The day that gave birth to all we are and all we do as Christians is like a forgotten stepchild.

How can we ensure that there are *three* big celebrations each year instead of only two? Mangers? Yes. Easter lilies? Certainly. But how can the wind and fire and languages of Pentecost become central for us as Christians, not marginal or ignored?

Part of the problem is that there is only one red Sunday in the year. When red is given less than 2 percent of our church calendar, it's no surprise that the Day of Pentecost fades into the shadows. Another part of the problem is that music for Pentecost Sunday is woefully scarce. For every 100 well-known Christmas songs there are perhaps a dozen well-known Easter songs and only a tiny

---

116 See Acts 2:5-11.

handful of songs for Pentecost.[117] Our creative musicians need to focus on red-letter music.

But until the theology of Pentecost is more widely understood, not much will happen to restore our half-forgotten celebration to prominence. One of my creative friends, Loretta Stein, taught me that red is the unifying color that runs through all of the purple and white and green seasons. The Holy Spirit, she pointed out, is present during the purple times of Advent and Lent, making us restless and hungry for the God of life and hope. In the same way, the Spirit is the source of our white season surprises and "exceeding great joy."[118] The green seasons, too, are times when God's Spirit is at work in us, energizing our labor, giving us a vision of a new world and a new me. Why, then, do we isolate our one red-letter Sunday from the other 51 or 52 Sundays in the year? Can't we invite God's Spirit to fall afresh on us in every season, revitalizing us and making sense of all we do as people of faith?

C. A RED-LETTER AWARENESS IN ME

The light bulb went on for me in my mid-life years. I began to see—not all at once, but gradually—that the seasons of the church years are identical to the seasons of my soul. The colors of faith provide

---

117 There are hopeful signs. Several new songs for Pentecost are now widely sung, especially "Spirit, Spirit of Gentleness," lyrics and music by James K. Manley, and "Spirit Song," lyrics and music by John Wimber. There are some old favorites as well: "Spirit of the Living God," lyrics and music by Daniel Iverson, and the African-American spiritual, "Every Time I Feel the Spirit."

118 Matthew 2:10 KJV describes the response of the Magi to the Star of Bethlehem: "They were filled with exceeding great joy." The Easter surprise is equally joy-filled. See, for example, the experience of Cleopas and his traveling companion when they realize that their dinner guest has been the Risen Christ. "Were not our hearts burning within us while he was talking to us on the road, while he was opening the Scriptures to us?" they say to each other in Luke 24:32. A strangely warmed heart is a sign of the Holy Spirit's presence.

CHAPTER 5. RED

a spiritual map for me and for all of us who are "Christians on the way."[119] The color red represents the Holy Spirit, present in every season. During my Advent times, the Holy Spirit was drawing me toward Christ, even though I was trying to run away. I was a young college student and later a lieutenant in the Army, determined to be self-sufficient. I kept churches (and God) at arm's length. "I'll think about religion," I said during those years of purple, "but I won't give up my autonomy. I won't let God be in charge of my life." It was a time of wandering for me, a time of spiritual confusion.

The Holy Spirit was also at work when God became real in my life—more than just a word. It was Christmas for me, a white season of comfort and joy. After singing "Joy to the World" for so many years without understanding the good news, I finally saw the Christ Child as a gift *for me*. Thanks to the Spirit that guides us into all truth, I was awake and alive as a newborn Christian.

Then came a new experience, made possible by the Holy Spirit. I began to feel a strong desire to study, to learn more about my faith in Christ. It was a green season of Epiphany for me, as I set out on the pathway of discipleship. The energy and the motivation came from God's red-letter gift.

Unfortunately, I imagined that active disciples were 100 percent faithful. And so I tried to be 100 percent strong and confident (or at least I pretended to be). How mistaken I was! When I was blindsided by several people I pastored, people who said they were disappointed in my leadership (some said I was too liberal,

---

[119] I have always been intrigued with the name of the early Christian movement. First-century believers described themselves as followers of "the Way" (Acts 9:2, 22:4). So it is with us today. As long as we live, we will be "on the way." We are disciples who have not fully arrived.

others that I was too conservative), I found myself in a new season of purple, a personal season of Lent. I struggled to understand the criticism and with the help of trusted colleagues began to discern how I could be more faithful to Christ, less fearful of public opinion. Those were painful days. But the Holy Spirit's presence, represented by the color red, helped me confront my people-pleasing tendencies and grow as a pastor. Repentance is never fun, but it's part of the curriculum for Christians. Always.

Eventually, the Spirit brought me back to a season of alleluias. "I will raise you up," God seemed to be saying, "not because of your own skills or cleverness. I will raise you up because I can speak through you and love through you and provide leadership through you, now that you have been humbled and broken." It was Easter for me. I knew that I was serving a risen Savior and that all was well.

I was ready to labor on, without worrying so much about my own success. I felt a new sense of liberation and began to experience glad surprises. I was discovering that God could work through me and in spite of me. One of my happiest experiences was teaching seminary classes as an adjunct faculty member. I was also delighted to travel to Nashville, our church's national headquarters, so that I could introduce a Spanish-language immersion program to leaders across America. In my local congregation I began to enjoy tasks that had been burdensome for me: raising funds to renovate our 75-year-old building; joining with teenagers on mission trips, including a trip to Tanzania; and building alliances with leaders from other faith traditions, especially Muslims in Chicago. What I learned was life-changing: the red-letter Day of Pentecost is more than a single Sunday on the church calendar. It is a red-letter experience that gives us a big-picture view of our life with Christ. The color red reminds us that God's best gift is present in every season, the gift of "I am with you now" to bless you with holy wisdom, holy power, and holy love.[120]

D. THEOLOGY IN THE COLOR RED

HERE AND NOW

The Holy Spirit is God in the present tense. God the Creator is beyond time and space, neither past nor present nor future (as human beings understand time) nor confined to a specific geographic location. God the Son, by contrast, is known to us through the life of a historical figure, Jesus of Nazareth. "He is the image of the invisible God," we are told in Colossians 1:15, which means that when we look at Jesus, we can begin to see and understand the Eternal Mystery. But if Jesus lived and died in the past and if the God of creation is always beyond time and space, how can we enter into a present-day, life-giving relationship with the Holy One? It is the Spirit, also known in Scripture as the Counselor or Advocate or Comforter or Helper,[121] who makes God real and accessible for us at every moment.

This is not a trivial statement. Without the Holy Spirit, we would be disconnected from the living God. We could admire Jesus, as we admire Shakespeare or Gandhi, but Christ would not be a

---

120 There can be many Advent times for us, along with numerous Christmas surprises. Epiphany, Lent, Easter, and Pentecost are not one-time experiences either. We can move through all of the seasons again and again, learning to repent in the times of purple, learning to receive God's amazing grace (with head and heart) in seasons of white, and learning to grow as a follower of Jesus when green is the color of our faith. Our personal seasons are not orderly or predictable. But the colors can help us find our way, giving us a biblical and theological framework for our spiritual journey.

121 See, for example, John 14:16, 26; 15:26.

living presence in our life. We could be amazed at the grandeur of the night sky, but there would be no intimate or personal relationship with the One who devised the Big Bang billions of years ago and who continues to know every star by name.[122] It is the Holy Spirit who makes God present now. The key word is *now*. If God matters to us at all, it is because the Spirit is bringing us into immediate contact with the One who is and was and is to come. No Holy Spirit means dead religion. Openness to the Holy Spirit means vital faith that can transform the world.

JOHN WESLEY AND THE HOLY SPIRIT

Wesley reaffirmed the Protestant understanding of grace, taught by Luther and the 16th-century Reformers: God forgives us and adopts us as sons and daughters, not because we have purchased God's love in any way, but simply because God allows the pain and death we deserve to fall upon Christ, that is, upon God's own person. This insight by Martin Luther was a return to Paul's teaching in the New Testament. It is solely by grace, Paul affirms, that we are pardoned by God and blessed with a new life of spiritual abundance.[123] If we were to donate $100,000 to build a church or to feed starving children in Somalia, God would love us no more than God already does. Our good behavior or lack of good behavior does not change the fact that "God so loved the world that he gave his only Son" (John 3:16). Nor do our deeds of generosity earn "heavenly reward points" for us. If I had four sons, two of whom

---

122 Psalm 147:4, Isaiah 40:26.

123 See, for example, Romans 3:28 and Ephesians 2:8.

CHAPTER 5. RED

were hard-working and two of whom were derelicts, I would be saddened by the lifestyle choices of the ones who were floundering, but if I were a good father, I would love them nonetheless. I would do nothing to coddle them. I would allow them to feel the painful consequences of their behavior. But I would continue to claim them as my children and do everything in my power to convince them: you are precious in my sight, and honored, and I love you.[124] This is how God loves each of us.

And it is a love that never changes. On Good Friday God bore the pain of our abandoning Jesus. But even as we cried out, "Crucify him!" God's compassion for us remained as strong as ever. We were breaking the heart of God, and yet God answered the prayer of Jesus on the cross: "Father, forgive them, for they do not know what they are doing" (Luke 23:34). We were not cast aside forever by the Judge of the universe. We were declared worthy sons and daughters, in spite of our unworthy track record. We were acquitted, so that our sins and failures were no longer part of our permanent record. "As far as the east is from the west, so far he removes our transgressions from us" (Psalm 103:12). This is too good to believe, we are tempted to say, but it is what Christians have affirmed as the gospel truth: "In the name of Jesus Christ you are forgiven!"[125]

And so the question is always: "Do I believe it? Do I believe this astonishing good news?" My ability to say, "Yes, I believe," is made possible by the Holy Spirit, who convinces me that I am

---

[124] These very words are spoken to the people of Israel, as they endure the pain of exile in Babylon. See Isaiah 43:4.

[125] This declaration is often used by United Methodists in the Basic Pattern of Worship. See *The United Methodist Hymnal* (1989), 2–11.

God's forgiven and beloved child.[126] God is offering us a love that is never-ending, never-failing, and unconditional, to which we can respond (as the Spirit empowers us): "Thank you, God! Yes!"

But grace is more than forgiveness. Grace is also the energizing power that transforms forgiven sinners into mature disciples. "By grace you have been saved," we are told in Ephesians 2:5. Are we saved from past sins only to continue living in darkness? "No!" John Wesley declared with fervor and passion. God's intention is to save us thoroughly, completely, entirely, so that we are not only pardoned but empowered to live more and more like Christ.[127]

This is the heart of Wesleyan theology: the grace of God as a powerful change agent. Grace, Wesley believed, is the Holy Spirit in action,[128] convincing us that we belong to God through Christ (justification) and changing us to make us truly Christlike (sanctification).

The link between grace and the Holy Spirit can be clearly seen in the colors of faith. In our purple seasons prevenient grace is the work of the Spirit, making us feel hollow and restless. In our white seasons justifying grace is also the work of the Spirit, blessing us with pardon and peace. In our green seasons sanctifying grace is at work, recreating us, reshaping our heart and mind and daily habits, renovating all that is shabby within us and inspiring us not

---

126 Romans 8:16 was one of John Wesley's favorite texts: "[T]hat very Spirit bear[s] witness with our spirit that we are children of God."

127 Wesley preached from the Book of Hebrews more than from any other book in the Bible. Hebrews 7:25 was a key text for him: "He is able also to save them to the uttermost that come unto God by him [Christ]" (KJV).

128 For a more complete description of Wesley's theology of grace, see W. Kirk Reed, *Reclaiming a Theological Heritage: John Wesley's Theology and Covenant Discipleship Groups in the United Methodist Church* (Unpublished doctoral project, Northern Baptist Theological Seminary, 1996).

only to attempt great things for God but also to do small things for God, always with great love.

Wesley's famous analogy describes repentance (purple) as the porch, justification (white) as the door, and sanctification (green) as the house, the house of the Lord where we are invited to live with God forever (Psalm 23:6). The color red symbolizes the Spirit that pokes and prods when we are outside, embraces us as we enter, and leads us onward as we become more mature as disciples.

THE HEALING OF THE NATIONS

Personal growth is where healthy religion begins. It's true, I believe, that you can't make a good omelet by using rotten eggs. Nor can you create a good society by starting with people who are spiritually dysfunctional. Jesus knew that whatever is in our heart will appear in our behavior.[129] And so spiritual renewal in societies and nations can never bypass spiritual renewal in individuals.

But personal growth is never the final goal of spiritual renewal. God's ultimate goal is a new Jerusalem,[130] a healthy community where peace prevails, not only in our hearts but also in the world that God loves. The day will come, says the Lord, when our tumultuous planet will be transformed into a peaceable kingdom.[131]

John Wesley's vision of holiness was 100 percent personal, but it was also 100 percent social. Personal holiness can become self-absorbed religiosity if it is focused solely on "me and God." True followers of Christ, Wesley believed, will care for the well-being

---

129 Matthew 15:11–19.
130 Revelation 21:1–2.
131 See, for example, Isaiah 11:6–9; 65:25.

of others, opposing social evils as well as caring for individuals. In 18th-century England, Wesley's Methodists vigorously opposed the slave trade. Today there are new social ills to confront.

All of God's creation is to be restored. The church is not like Noah's ark, a place to hide and huddle together, while the planet is being destroyed by floods of hedonism and hatefulness. Within our democratic system, where many points of view are constantly competing, we can—we must—listen to each other and learn from each other. Together we can achieve small victories that can never be accomplished by one-sided trashing of Republicans by Democrats or total rejection of Democrats by Republicans.

Again, God's dream is for a just and peaceful world. We may not see it in our lifetime, but it remains God's dream. Can we "bring in the kingdom" by our faltering human efforts? No. (There have been times, of course, when Christian reformers have been overconfident, claiming that the kingdom of God was at hand. In my grandparents' lifetime, the Great War of 1914–1918 dashed all such hopes.) But as each of us responds to the Spirit of God symbolized by the color red, and as we team up with others who are called to work for authentic and enduring shalom, there can be small steps of progress.

God promises to provide a stream of living water that will flow through a new heaven and a new earth (Revelation 22:1–2). On either side of the stream, which symbolizes the flow of the Holy Spirit, there will be a tree of life that can heal our planet. "And the leaves of the tree are for the healing of the nations" (v. 2). "So may it be, O Lord," we pray, inviting God to use each of us to make the dream a reality.

CHAPTER 5. RED

QUESTIONS FOR DISCUSSION

1. Has the Holy Spirit been central to your life of faith, or has the Holy Spirit been half-forgotten and peripheral?

2. If grace is the Holy Spirit in action, disturbing (in purple seasons), reassuring (in white seasons), and empowering (in green seasons), how can we be more open to God's grace? How can we allow the Holy Spirit to fill us, so that we will not suffer from a power shortage in the church?

3. Has your church been able to keep personal holiness and social holiness in balance, or has one been overemphasized at the expense of the other? Is it wise to care for individuals without also caring about social issues, such as education, crime, taxes, immigration, jobs, and war?

4. Does the movement from purple to white to green—empowered by red—make sense to you? Do you agree that all Christians experience seasons of the soul: seasons of sadness, seasons of joy, and seasons of grateful discipleship?

Chapter 6. SMALL, BIG, AND GREAT QUESTIONS

There are small questions that many of us care about, such as: "Who makes the best smart phone?" or "Will the Arizona Wildcats ever play in the Rose Bowl?" They are small questions because no matter how we answer them, they will not make us permanently happy or unhappy.

Other questions are big by comparison, such as: "How can we improve our public schools in America?" or "Are we poisoning our future with greenhouse gases?" The answers will definitely affect our long-term happiness.

There is a third category of questions that I call the Great Questions. They are great in that they are enduring, like the perennial Great Books. The questions have been asked by human beings in every culture and in every period of history. If we are old enough to wonder who we are and why we are here, we are old enough to search for the answers.

Those who claim to be non-religious cannot avoid the questions. Their answers may be quite different from those given by a Buddhist or Hindu or Christian or Muslim or Jew. But it is impossible to say "The questions don't exist." Everyone above a certain age—even the least philosophical and least religious—has a position, an outlook, a way of answering.

There are four Great Questions that *The Colors of Faith* can help us answer.

1. Do we have a destination?
2. Do we have a map?
3. Do we have a means of transportation?
4. Do we want to make the journey?

This final question is different from the others, because it requires a personal decision, a leap of faith. If a train is leaving the station, we can decide to be on board, or we can decide to remain on the platform. If we refuse to decide, we have made a definite decision.

DO WE HAVE A DESTINATION?

Lewis Carroll, author of *Alice in Wonderland*, reminds us in a charming way that destinations matter. "If you don't know where you are going," he says, "any road will get you there." The world's major religions speak of ultimate destinations, using symbolic language—words like "paradise" or "sheol" or "hell" or "nirvana"—to describe what is beyond our everyday experience. There are foretastes or previews in this life, but the full experience is in the future.

Are all major religions essentially the same? Are they all pointing toward the same destination? Definitely not, says Stephen Prothero, Professor of Religion at Boston University. "The world's religious rivals do converge when it comes to ethics, but they diverge

CHAPTER 6. SMALL, BIG, AND GREAT QUESTIONS

sharply on doctrine, ritual, mythology, experience, and law."[132] They differ as well in describing our ultimate goal or destination.

Every religion, Prothero says, begins with a simple observation: something is wrong with the world. Every religion then offers a solution. For Christians the goal is salvation from sin. For Confucianists the goal is character development, so that social chaos can be controlled. For Buddhists is goal is quite different: release from the "ignorant craving" that underlies all human suffering. For this to occur, Buddhists believe, the human self must be extinguished. For Muslims the goal is surrender: surrender of our willful selves to the one God whose will is perfect.

Do we have a destination? This is not simply a religious question. It is a human question. The New Atheists who despise religion are proposing an answer, declaring that our ultimate destination is non-existence, the dissolution of the human body as it returns to the earth. The world's religions, by contrast, offering openings "through which the inexhaustible energies of the cosmos enter human life." In this way, says Huston Smith, religion can "inspire life's deepest creative centers".[133] Yes, Smith freely admits, religious faith has been and will continue to be perverted. In every religion there are unhealthy beliefs and practices. (Someone has jokingly suggested that the biggest mistake religion ever made was to get mixed up with people!) But healthy religion, as Oliver Wendell Holmes was fond of saying, is at work on the things that matter most. Its successes are small at times, but religion offers meaningful

---

132 Stephen Prothero, *God Is Not One* (New York: HarperOne, 2010), 3.
133 Huston Smith, *The World's Religions* (San Francisco: Harper, 1991), 9.

answers to the Great Questions. One of the essential questions will always be: "Do we have a destination?"

How have Christians answered this question through the centuries? In the traditional language of Scripture, the goal is salvation—more specifically, salvation from sin and death. For some Christians this has been an otherworldly goal. "Heaven is our home" has been their mantra. Therefore, earthly concerns seem trivial be comparison. Other Christians have argued that otherworldliness is a mistake. The real goal, they have said, is salvation or well-being for all people in this life. Poverty, disease, and violence are more important concerns than "pie in the sky by and by". A more balanced view, I believe, is to take heaven seriously, while insisting that Jesus came to transform the physical world as well. Yes, heaven is our ultimate home, but the heavenly banquet begins in this life, we are told in the New Testament, as we live in Christ and as Christ lives in us.[134]

What does it mean for God's will to be done on earth? How can salvation be described in a way that makes sense in our everyday life? The Bible offers a colorful array of symbols and metaphors, described in Chapter 3. To be saved is to live with confidence and clarity; to be healthy in all of our relationships; to experience life to the full, as we serve a higher purpose; to become more like Christ. These are significant goals. Christians believe that they are worthy of our highest devotion. They remind us that faith is a colorful, adventure-filled journey—in this life and in the life to come.

---

134 John 14:23, John 16:22, Romans 6:4, II Corinthians 5:17, Colossians 3:1.

CHAPTER 6. SMALL, BIG, AND GREAT QUESTIONS

DO WE HAVE A MAP?

Every Muslim knows what to do in order to please Allah: pray five times daily, give generously to the poor (2.5% of total assets), make a pilgrimage to Mecca, fast during the month of Ramadan, and confess that there is one God and that Muhammed is God's messenger. In a similar way, there is a clear pathway that Buddhists are to follow: a Noble Eightfold Path that offers release from ignorance and self-concern.

But what map do Christians follow? Most Christians receive guidance that is vague at best. The instructions are: "Attend worship. Pray. Read the Bible. Love your neighbor. Give generously." But how? What does it mean to worship in a profound way? Is it enough to sit in a pew at worship, or is more required? How should we pray? Once a day or before meals or constantly? Is it better to use a prescribed prayer, or should we offer spontaneous prayers? Where do we begin, if we want to make sense of the Bible? How can interpret the passages that are difficult and confusing? What does it mean to love our neighbor? And what is meant by generous giving? Is tithing required (10% of our income), or is the amount optional?

The Roman Catholic Church has had clear rules through the centuries, including dietary rules (no meat on Fridays), rules for sexual relationships (no "unnatural" birth control), and rules for participating in the Eucharist (no communion without proper confession and absolution). But many Christians today long for a more wholistic approach to the Christian life. They are hoping to find a spiritual map that can guide them without being rigid or coercive.

In fact, Christians do have such a map. It does not bind us to a legalistic set of practices. There is room for individual choice and variation, which is appropriate, since every Christian has a unique story. But the map orients us. It tells us where we have been, where we are now, and what we can expect in the future. It suggests positive steps that we can take to move ahead in our spiritual journey. It warns us of dead ends and dangers. It keeps us focused and on track.

The map uses four colors that have guided Christians through the centuries. The three basic colors represent stages or seasons in our journey with Christ. **Purple** is the first color of faith. In purple seasons we are waiting and struggling. No one, no matter how faithful or devoted, can escape the color purple. **White** is the second color of faith. In white seasons all is well, and there is unspeakable joy. **Green** is the third color of faith. In green seasons we gratefully accept the challenges God places before us, challenges to grow and serve as disciples. Is it hard work? Yes. But it is good work, satisfying work that leaves us feeling rewarded and blessed. **Red** is the fourth color of faith, representing the Spirit of God, the One who leads us through the times of purple, white, and green. Red symbolizes the means of transportation for all who follow Christ.

Because we are not generic Christians or carbon copies of each other, the colors do not force us into a lockstep pattern of religion. The colors simply tell us: "There are seasons of the soul, and every Christian—new believers and long-time disciples, high church Anglicans and low church Baptists, those who love Christ and those who are searching and struggling, everyone!—can benefit from having a time-tested map. Without a map we can wander aimlessly. But when we have a dependable map, we can find our way to the place that God has prepared for us (John 14:3), the place that Christians call "home".

CHAPTER 6. SMALL, BIG, AND GREAT QUESTIONS

DO WE HAVE A MEANS OF TRANSPORTATION?

If I wanted to climb Mount Everest, I would have an exciting destination. There are excellent maps that I could follow. But the question would remain: how would I be traveling? Would I travel by plane or helicopter to the top of Everest? Definitely not. Would I be carried on someone's back or hauled on a litter? For a short distance, perhaps, but not to the summit. The only sure means of transportation would be foot power: putting one foot in front of another.

The spiritual journey of a Christian is also exciting—and demanding. "Through many dangers, toils, and snares I have already come; 'tis grace has brought me safe thus far, and grace will lead me home."[135] The former captain of a British slave ship, John Newton wrote these familiar words in the year 1779. He was describing the one sure means of transportation for Christians. It is not self-generated power. It is Spirit power, or more simply: amazing grace.

Grace is the power that transforms us from solitary individuals ("it's all about me") to partners with God ("it's all about joining with others to repair the world"). Grace is God's constant favor. Grace is the source of every talent and skill that we possess. Grace, in short, is the Spirit of the living God, freely offered to each of us—with no strings attached—so that we can thrive and help others thrive.

But grace without discipline is like seeds in a package, never planted, inert, unable to grow. Grace without discipline is like jet fuel in a storage tank, never empowering a liftoff. By discipline I

---

135 John Newton, "Amazing Grace," verse 3.

mean intentional effort: (1) to know God's will, and (2) to do what God desires. The place to begin is to study the map that God provides for us, the map of purple, white, and green, empowered by red.

If we are in a purple season of life, God's **prevenient grace** is making us restless and unsatisfied. If we are in a white season, God's **justifying grace** has set us free from guilt and fear. If we are in a green season, God's **sanctifying grace** is stirring us and prodding us and calling us to "make disciples of Jesus Christ for the transformation of the world".[136]

John Wesley realized that grace is far more than God's forgiveness, extended to unworthy strugglers. Grace is also energy and power, goodness from beyond ourselves that changes us forever. If I fail to study for my chemistry exam and receive a low D-minus, my professor may decide to forgive my poor performance, telling me: "I won't count the D-minus against you." That would be wonderful news. But what if she tells me that next Thursday, one week from today, I will be given a new test? I may panic, especially if my chemistry skills are shaky. But here is the best news of all. She tells me: "I am willing to meet with you every afternoon between now and next Thursday, and I can help you pull up your grade." What could be more encouraging? "I will not only forgive you," she is saying. "I will help you grow and learn."

It's the same promise that God makes to each of us in the areas where we are struggling. "I will not only forgive you for your past failures," God says, "but I will work with you for as long as it takes, so that you can succeed—with flying colors. You will need to meet

---

136 United Methodist Mission Statement, 2012.

CHAPTER 6. SMALL, BIG, AND GREAT QUESTIONS

with me, though. You will need to study and apply yourself. I won't do it *for* you, but I will do it *with* you." The secret is disciplined grace, combined with graceful discipline.

Every major religion of the world offers a means of transportation. Only the Christian faith offers unlimited grace, available for everyone who is thirsty, "without money and without price" (Isaiah 55:1).

WILL I SAY YES TO THE JOURNEY?

This question is in some ways the simplest of all: "Will we say yes to the journey? Will we take a leap of faith into the unknown, or will we hesitate, holding back?" There are some who decide: "I'm not ready to follow this map or use this means of transportation. In fact, I'm not convinced that this destination is for me.

When I visit Niagara Falls, I remember the tightrope walkers. The first to attempt the crossing was Jean Francois Gravelet, known professionally as "The Great Blondin." At the age of 31 Blondin came to America and made a dramatic announcement: "I will cross the entire gorge of the Niagara River on a tightrope." At 5:00 pm on June 30, 1859, he made history, not only crossing the falls but doing a backward somersault while approaching the Canadian shore. Later he accomplished the feat blindfolded. The tale is told that before one of his crossings, he challenged the hordes of people who had come to watch and be amazed: "Does anyone here believe I can walk across with a wheelbarrow?" Everyone cheered and offered encouragement. Then he smiled and said: "If you really believe it, will one of you climb into the wheelbarrow?"

Everything changes when our life is on the line. Suddenly we are no longer spectators. We are no longer passive observers. And so the question is always before us: do we want to make the journey of faith, following the way of Jesus?

"Come, follow me," says Jesus. He doesn't say: "Sit and watch." I used to have a sign in my bedroom, when I was a teenager: "Work fascinates me; I can sit and watch it for hours." Church folks can sit and watch for years, professing to be attracted to Jesus but never answering "Yes," when he calls us to follow.

The Christian journey is not easy. The color of our faith can be dishearteningly purple. Yes, there are white seasons of exuberant joy, but the exhilaration eventually fades. We find ourselves at work again, in a green season that can test us to the breaking point.

Why would anyone say yes to a journey that is precarious and demanding? No one said yes to the Great Blondin, when he invited spectators to climb into his wheelbarrow. Is it any different for us, when we are invited by Jesus to "take up [our] cross and follow" (Matthew 16:24)? The good news is this: instead of calling us to cross the Niagara gorge, Jesus is inviting us to embark on a wondrous journey: from darkness to light, from brokenness to well-being, from black-and-white blandness to vibrant, abundant life—in living color. The offer is on the table for each of us.

Christians believe that God can carry us safely through the dangers, toils, and snares and that there will be glad surprises along the way. The destination is of supreme worth. The map is clear and dependable. The means of transportation—grace and more grace—are freely offered to everyone. Only one question remains. Will we say yes to the journey?

CHAPTER 6. SMALL, BIG, AND GREAT QUESTIONS

QUESTIONS FOR DISCUSSION

1. What, if anything, is unique about the Christian faith? How would you respond to someone who says, "All religions are the same"?

2. Reading a travel guide about France is different from walking through the streets of Paris. In the same way, reading Bible stories about Jesus is different from traveling through life at Jesus' side. Can you think of times in your life when "head faith" became "whole person faith," when the idea of following Christ became a living reality?

3. Which of the Great Questions are most interesting or thought-provoking for you? Do the colors of the Christian faith—purple, white, green, and red—provide answers that are helpful?

PURPLE	
The feeling of purple	**SADNESS**
The idea of purple	**STRUGGLE AND PAIN**
The direction of purple	**SINKING**
The theology of purple	**SIN**

THE PURPLE SEASONS		
	ADVENT	**LENT**
In the Christian year	4 Sundays	40 days + 6 Sundays
In the church's story	Waiting for a Savior	Rejecting the Savior
In Scripture	Old Testament	Gospels—Near the end
In my personal story	Feeling lost, dissatisfied	Failing, falling away
Our response in times of purple	**REPENTANCE or DENIAL**	

CHAPTER 6. SMALL, BIG, AND GREAT QUESTIONS

WHITE	
The feeling of white	JOY
The idea of white	ALL IS WELL
The direction of white	TURNING
The theology of white	NEW BIRTH, JUSTIFICATION BY FAITH
THE WHITE SEASONS	

	CHRISTMAS	EASTER
In the Christian year	12 Days (December 25–January 5)	7 Weeks (Beginning Easter Sunday)
In the church's story	Jesus is born	Jesus is raised to life
In Scripture	Gospels—Beginning	Gospels—End
In my personal story	A new relationship with God, a new life of freedom and purpose	Forgiveness, a new beginning after failing and falling away
Our response in times of white	**FAITH or SELF-RELIANCE**	

GREEN	
The feeling of green	GRATEFULNESS
The idea of green	RESILIENT GROWING
The direction of green	RISING
The theology of green	SANCTIFICATION, BECOMING LIKE CHRIST

THE GREEN SEASONS		
	EPIPHANY	PENTECOST
In the Christian year	January 6–Mardi Gras	23–27 weeks after the Day of Pentecost
In the church's story	Jesus's ministry of teaching and healing	Christ's ministry through the church
In Scripture	Gospels—Middle	Acts through Revelation
In my personal story	Learning to follow Jesus	Witnessing and serving
Our response in times of green	GRACEFUL DISCIPLINE or APATHY/COMPULSIVENESS	

CHAPTER 6. SMALL, BIG, AND GREAT QUESTIONS

	RED
The feeling of red	**AWE AND WORSHIP**
The idea of red	**GOD'S HOLY PRESENCE**
The direction of red	**SINKING/TURNING/RISING**
The theology of red	**GRACE IN EVERY PERSON**
• In purple seasons	Prevenient grace
• In white seasons	Justifying grace
• In green seasons	Sanctifying grace
THE RED LETTER SUNDAY	
In the Christian year	**THE DAY OF PENTECOST** The 50th day after Easter
In the church's story	God's wisdom, power, and love available for all people
In Scripture	Acts 1–2
In my personal story	God in the present tense
Our response to the gift of God's Spirit	**RECEIVING or RESISTING**

ACKNOWLEDGEMENTS

As a child sitting through Sunday morning sermons, I looked at the colors on the altar and I wondered "Why? Why do the colors keep changing?" I had no idea that the colors were telling a story. Or rather, the procession of Purple, White, Green, and Red were telling three stories:

1. The Biblical story from Genesis to Revelation
2. The personal story of Christians (including me) in every century
3. The theological story that provides meaning for our daily life

Two books made the colors—and their stories—come alive for me. The first was a small book by David G. Owen, *Transparent Worship*. It summarized in a clear and profound way what the liturgical colors are saying, if we are paying attention. The second book was *Theology in the Wesleyan Spirit* by Albert C. Outler. I literally fell in love with John Wesley's theology after feasting on Outler's four-chapter summary, and chapters 2, 3, and 4 showed me that Purple, White, and Green are precisely the key theological concepts that Wesley taught and preached.

But theology is of little value if it is unrelated to our everyday life, and so I am deeply grateful to the United Methodist congregations I served in the Chicago area. They helped me make Wesley's theology practical and even exciting at times. They wanted to feel the colors and the seasons of the church year instead of merely hearing about them. I was deepened and enriched by each congregation: Berry Memorial (Chicago); North Northfield (Northbrook); Sycamore (Sycamore); Trinity (Mount Prospect); and Trinity (Wilmette).

Two mentors led me on an inward journey that brought me into a desperately needed intimacy with the Holy One. They transformed my life and my ministry. Rev. Bill Obalil and Rev. Dr. Hal Edwards will always be among my most admired teachers and fellow pilgrims.

Here in Tucson I have been greatly encouraged by Donna Celenza-Sweet, Carol and Neil West, Ellie Patterson, Michael Drake, Bob DeLaney, Bob Grady, Francine Rienstra, and the remarkable members of the Koinonia Class at Catalina United Methodist Church—and many others who have stood with me in the Purple seasons of sorrow as well as in the White seasons of great gladness.

Andrea Coens is *La Suprema* in the art and skill of proofreading. She helped me in every way to prepare a manuscript that surpasses my early efforts. *Mil gracias, mi amiga.*

My amazing children—Bryan, Daniel, and Katie—and their families continue to inspire me. They make me want to be a better dad and a more loving grandpa. Daniel used his computer skills in masterful ways to prepare *The Colors of Faith* for publication.

A word of confession. There were times during 40 years of professional ministry when I failed to challenge the laypeople who attended faithfully. They were looking for Biblical and theological depth, and like many pastors I sometimes offered ecclesiastical baby food. I hope that this book can help compensate for the times when I didn't go deep enough.

Theology alone won't save the church or the world, but when combined with hearts on fire with love for God and for our neighbors—including our ever-present neighbor, the planet Earth—theology can strengthen us and make us wiser and bolder as followers of Jesus.

Made in the USA
Columbia, SC
16 July 2021